TEACHERS WHO ARE
BLIND OR VISUALLY IMPAIRED

JOBS THAT MATTER

An engaging series written by Deborah Kendrick and devoted to the personal stories of individuals who are blind or visually impaired and who are successful in fields of work they have chosen, *Jobs That Matter* profiles inspiring role models for blind and visually impaired students who want to achieve satisfaction in the world of work.

TITLES IN THE JOBS THAT MATTER SERIES
Teachers Who Are Blind or Visually Impaired

ALSO AVAILABLE FROM AFB PRESS
Jobs To Be Proud Of: Profiles of Workers Who Are Blind or Visually Impaired
Career Perspectives: Interviews with Blind and Visually Impaired Professionals

JOBS THAT MATTER

Teachers Who Are Blind or Visually Impaired

Deborah Kendrick

PRESS

New York

Printed in the United States of America

Library of Congress Cataloging-in-Publication Data
Kendrick, Deborah, 1950-
    Teachers who are blind or visually impaired / Deborah Kendrick.
      p. cm.
    (Jobs That Matter series) ISBN 0-89128-306-4 (lg. print : pbk. : alk. paper)
    1. Blind teachers—United States—Biography. 2. Visually
handicapped teachers—United States—Biography. I. Title.
II. Series.
[HV1623.K45 1998]
371.1'0092'2—dc21   98-14687
[B]   CIP

The preface by Dr. Fredric K. Schroeder that appears in this volume was written in his personal capacity and his remarks do not necessarily reflect the position of the U.S. Department of Education.

CONTENTS

FOREWORD

I N 1990, the American Foundation for the Blind (AFB) published a book entitled *Career Perspectives*, which profiled individuals who are blind or visually impaired to serve as possible role models for young people with visual impairments and the people who lived and worked with them. The book was intended to offer a wide range of possibilities for young people who aspire to professional careers. Given AFB's ongoing concern about the vital issues affecting the lives of blind and visually impaired persons in this country, in 1993 we continued to pursue issues related to young people and employment in collaboration with Deborah Kendrick, an award-winning journalist who is blind, with the publication of *Jobs To Be Proud Of*. This book contained a series of engaging profiles of workers who enjoyed what they did and who were performing jobs that did not require advanced academic training for success. Both books were designed to provide young blind and visually impaired people with descriptions of inspiring personal experiences that might help them in their own approach to choosing a career. Soon people from across the country were enthusiastically telling us at AFB how much they particularly enjoyed *Jobs To Be Proud Of* and how valuable a publication it was. In 1994, the book earned national recognition when the American Council of the Blind honored it with its Vernon Henley Media Award.

With the publication of *Teachers Who Are Blind or Visually Impaired,* we are pleased to announce the beginning of a series, Jobs That Matter, that follows up on *Jobs To Be Proud Of.* The success of that book in letting young people and their families and counselors, teachers, and other professionals who worked with them know about employment ideas and opportunities was gratifying to AFB and to Deborah Kendrick as well. The Jobs That Matter series is intended to demonstrate the wide variety of employment paths that blind and visually impaired people are successfully pursuing. Some of the career areas to be considered in the series include health care, art, computer technology, and business. In *Teachers Who Are Blind or Visually Impaired,* Kendrick introduces us to 18 educators whose inspiring stories reveal the tenacity of individuals who have successfully fulfilled their dreams of teaching. Although they vary in age and race and they are located throughout the United States, the teachers all share a devotion and enthusiasm for helping their students learn, and they show how it is possible to achieve classroom success and satisfaction in their work.

We at AFB believe that each book in the Jobs That Matter series will be an exceptionally valuable resource for children, adolescents, and adults who are blind or visually impaired and their families, teachers, guidance counselors, and employers. Because unemployment and underemployment are among the most serious problems facing persons who are blind or visually impaired today, it is important that young people are given support in the areas of self-esteem, career development, and finding and retaining jobs. We hope that the teachers portrayed in this book can serve as role models for visually impaired students who themselves may want to become teachers someday. And, we thank all the educators who agreed to be interviewed for this book, who provided photographs for it, and who shared their teaching experiences with us.

Carl R. Augusto
President
American Foundation for the Blind

PREFACE

THIS LATEST WORK by Deborah Kendrick is an important contribution to the body of literature documenting the ability of people who are blind or visually impaired to function competitively in a wide range of occupations. The efforts of blind people to seek employment in the teaching profession tell a story much greater than one that relates the ingenuity of determined people to find alternative methods for managing the myriad responsibilities associated with their jobs.

As a blind child, I did not automatically assume that I would be able to grow up and live a normal life pursuing my interests in the same way as others. When I graduated from college with a master's degree in education, I had never earned a paycheck of any kind. As a teenager, I never mowed a lawn, shoveled snow from a driveway, or delivered a newspaper. In college, I did not hold the typical part-time jobs flipping hamburgers or waiting on tables. Even though I had good grades and good recommendations from my instructors, when I sent out résumés, I can remember wondering whether I, as a blind person, could really do anything for which anyone would want to pay me. As a young teacher, I faced many challenges. I had to develop techniques for writing on the chalkboard, for grading papers, and for maintaining order in the classroom. I had to develop methods for preparing lessons, including overheads and handouts. Nevertheless, to solve these problems, I first had to believe in myself and believe that as a blind person I could teach effectively.

Achieving social integration is a process rooted in the interrelationship between skills and confidence. As blind people, we should have the skills we need to be competitive, the skills of braille reading and writing and the use of the long cane. But we should also have the confidence to put these skills into practice, for as we do, we reinforce our belief in our fundamental ability.

There are many ways people who are blind may gain this confidence. Some have supportive families and others have teachers and friends who encourage them and help them to believe in their ability to live integrated lives. Yet, I personally believe that all blind people can benefit significantly through association with other blind people. In my own life, I was fortunate in that a blind friend introduced me to the National Federation of the Blind. Through my association with other blind people, I gained a perspective of blindness much broader than I could otherwise have achieved. This experience helped me understand the importance of blind people working together to help reshape society's assumptions and beliefs about blindness and helped me understand the importance of blind people encouraging and supporting one another. I had people around me who believed in me more than I believed in myself and who encouraged me to seek out the training I needed to be able to function independently as a blind person.

The vignettes in this book tell an important story. They tell of blind and visually impaired people who have found the courage to withstand discrimination and who have found imaginative solutions to everyday problems. They tell of blind people who have gained confidence born of self-respect and who have taught society that blindness is no impediment to a full and rewarding career. Through their experiences, opportunities for blind people everywhere have been forever expanded, and through their stories, young people who are blind or visually impaired may be inspired to pursue their own interests and paths.

Fredric K. Schroeder, Ph.D.
Former Executive Director
New Mexico Commission for the Blind

ACKNOWLEDGMENTS

THERE WERE MANY JOYS in preparing this book, but perhaps the most rewarding was the eagerness to share and to help that greeted me from every quarter. I wish to acknowledge all the teachers profiled here for their patience with follow-up interviews and minutiae and their willingness to tell their stories. I also wish to thank the many, many talented teachers who are blind or visually impaired who are not in this book, for even though their names do not appear in these pages, their experiences helped me shape the text.

Jay Leventhal of the Careers and Technology Information Bank of the American Foundation for the Blind was a tireless source of ideas, as were both the professional teachers' organizations within the American Council of the Blind and the National Federation of the Blind.

In addition, I especially want to thank Fredric K. Schroeder, a recognized leader in the field of education for blind children, who is former Executive Director of the New Mexico Commission for the Blind and the current Commissioner of the Rehabilitation Services Administration, U.S. Department of Education. Whether he speaks as a blind person, as a talented teacher, or as an executive who has worked at the state and federal levels, he speaks with wisdom, and his preface is an appreciated addition to this book.

Acknowledgments would not be complete without expressing thanks to my editors, Natalie Hilzen and Kathy Campbell, who never wearied of making suggestions, reviewing pages, and gently directing my work—and, of course, to Catherine Brown, the first-grade teacher whom I recall in my introduction to this book and who made me believe that a blind child could grow up to do anything.

INTRODUCTION

WHEN I WAS SIX YEARS OLD, I fell in love. In love, that is, in the way only six-year-olds can—with open, boundless admiration, affection, and adoration for one particular grown-up. The recipient of this outpouring was my first-grade teacher, Mrs. Brown.

Mrs. Brown was like a mother, a best friend, a sports coach, and a no-nonsense governess all rolled into one. She taught me to read—in my case in braille—and I have always associated my love of words with my love for her.

I do not remember Mrs. Brown's ever telling me there was a single dream beyond my grasp. And that, I suspect, was why I loved her so much. She believed in my potential greatness, and somehow, without words, she communicated it to me every day I was in her care.

Throughout history, teachers have had powerful impacts on students, from preschool through graduate school. Many of those students have been blind or visually impaired, and many of their teachers have been, too.

The first gratifying thing I learned in preparing to write this book was that there are so many creative, capable, respected teachers who are blind or visually impaired in the United States. Choosing which ones would appear in these pages was no easy task, and they should not be viewed, by any means, as the only inspiring examples. They are, instead, a sampling of the rich variety of teachers who are blind or visually impaired who can serve as role models and mentors for others to follow.

All the teachers in these pages have been successful in fulfilling their dreams of teaching. They are of different ages, races, and geographic locations, and their teaching experiences have varied. Their ways of dealing with blindness or visual impairment in the classroom are both surprisingly similar to and dramatically different from one another.

These teachers' range of interests beyond teaching varies just as much as their attitudes toward job accommodations. Some bring their passion for music, art, or sports to the classroom, whereas others are more duty bound to prescribed curricula. Some throw themselves into a multitude of after-school activities, while others lead a quiet life outside school. Why should one expect it to be otherwise? These teachers represent exactly the diversity found among those who are not blind or visually impaired.

As future teachers consult this book for direction and inspiration, they will get some sense of the educational and personal requirements of the job. Those specifications can be found in hundreds of books.

What is hard to find elsewhere is an account of the details that constitute a day's work for teachers who happen to be blind or visually impaired. How do teachers grade papers, identify students, and monitor the behavior of children when they cannot see or see well? These are the kinds of issues that are addressed in this book by people who are teaching in a variety of settings.

One recurring theme that connects these teachers to each other, as well as to all the other teachers who were interviewed but not included here, is the reality of discrimination in hiring. I heard the story again and again. Armed with their degrees, teaching credentials, and plenty of hope, these aspiring teachers left school only to find that they could not obtain interviews or, worse, that having experienced good interviews, they did not receive job offers. For most, the pattern was broken when one employer happened to know someone with another connection to the would-be teacher. For example, one college professor believes that because another competent blind person was well known on campus, he was given a fair interview and subsequent offer. For another, the presence of both blindness and racial minority status seemed to cancel each other out, so the teacher experienced no real discrimination.

The one ingredient for success that every teacher mentioned is the power of support from colleagues and administrators. For instance, when a mother threatened to pull her child out of school because the teacher, Melissa Williamson, was blind, the school's administrator stood staunchly by Williamson, expressing regret to the mother for the loss on both sides. Similarly, Christina Cooke maintains that she has rarely had disciplinary problems simply because the entire staff is so supportive of her and of one another that disrespect would not be tolerated.

Some teachers have had awkward moments on the job related to blindness or visual impairment. Like all other of life's awkward moments, they passed. For the most part, the experiences shared by the teachers in this book illustrate that with sufficient motivation and support, blind or visually impaired students should be able to grow up to be whatever they want to be. The stories these teachers tell are of days filled with the joy, humor, hard work, and creativity that come with imparting knowledge to others. Some of them even remind me of why I fell in love with Mrs. Brown so long ago.

Any student who happens to be blind or visually impaired and wants to teach should weigh the experiences of these teachers as part of the decision-making process. Whether these teachers have been singled out for recognition of excellence or, as Virgil Cook put it, are "just one of the herd," it is clear that perhaps because of their blindness or visual impairment, rather than in spite of it, they are all bringing something of immeasurable extra value to their classrooms.

—D. K.

PRESCHOOL-PRIMARY
GRADES

ABOUT MICHELLE ROGERS

HOME
Muscatine, Iowa

SCHOOL
Good Shepherd of the Cross Lutheran Preschool

AGE
34

CAUSE OF VISUAL IMPAIRMENT
Retinitis pigmentosa

VISUAL ACUITY
20/160 (6/48 [its metric equivalent]) in both eyes (reads regular or large print slowly and can see motion at close range)

PRESCHOOL DIRECTOR AND TEACHER

Michelle Rogers

"I love children. I just can't think of anything else I'd rather do."

UNTIL SHE WAS in the third grade, Michelle Rogers remembers reading regular print and having no difficulty seeing across the classroom. At about that time, however, her vision began to fail, and she was diagnosed with retinitis pigmentosa.

Today, her visual acuity is such that she can read printed materials with a Visualtek closed-circuit television and can use her home computer with a 17-inch (44-cm) monitor. Recorded textbooks from Recording for the Blind and Dyslexic helped get her through college and graduate school, she says, but she does not see well enough to drive a car.

To the three- and four-year-olds who are her daily charges, however, Rogers just needs to get close to see things. But, everyone gets close to three- and four-year-olds for teaching and interactive play.

"I knew by the end of my freshman year at Western Illinois University that I wanted to teach," recalls the former psychology major. "I liked children really well and thought that it was something I'd be good at doing."

Although her student teaching and practicum experiences were all positive, Rogers had difficulty landing a job. She had been in several honor societies, graduated with a 3.9 grade-point average, and had good recommendations, but there were no offers.

"When applications asked about handicaps," she says, "I always put down my legal blindness because I thought it was important to be honest. So employers would ask questions about it. I could never prove it, but I'm sure discrimination was an obstacle to my getting a job right out of school."

Rogers did substitute teaching for a while, worked part time in a day care center, and then returned to school. In 1988, she graduated from Southern Illinois University in Carbondale with a master's degree in educational psychology.

When Rogers and her husband moved from Illinois to Iowa, they became involved in their church, and Rogers's background in early childhood education became known to the pastor. Being visible and letting one's talents be known are tips offered by many career counselors, and they were indeed techniques that paid off for Michelle Rogers. The church had been informally considering the possibility of establishing a preschool, and it was not long before the pastor of her church approached his new parishioner with the concept. In September 1991, Rogers opened the doors to her first class.

She is both the director and master teacher of the preschool, working from 8 to 12 every morning and doing most of her planning at home in the afternoon. She teaches 21 children in all, 10 three-year-olds two mornings per week and 11 four-year-olds the other three mornings. Rogers is paid from the enrollment fees paid by parents, not directly by the church. Out of that income, she also pays for all teaching supplies and for her assistant.

"Part of the reason I went into preschool education is that everything is bigger and more colorful and easier to see," she comments in regard to handling the details of teaching. Rogers works with children in small groups, so she is able to see what each child is doing. What she cannot see (like a child pinching another child across the room) her assistant will.

To read stories to the children, she works with new books at home—reading, rehearsing, and memorizing. She holds the book in front of her, cued by bright pictures and some text, and "reads" the rest from memory.

Few of the students are actually members of the church in which the preschool is housed. Instead, parents hear of the school by word of mouth, and the fact that enrollment is always full is Rogers's best indicator that she is doing a good job. Parents are obviously recommending the school to their friends.

Once each month, Rogers meets with about 25 other Muscatine teachers of children in preschool through grade 3 to share art ideas and teaching techniques. "When you pay for your own supplies," she says, "you learn to be very cost effective and find the best places to buy construction paper and crayons!"

Rogers rides the Muscabus, a local paratransit service for people with disabilities, to and from school each day and points out that even though her students know she rides the bus, none has ever asked why. Otherwise, she has no special on-the-job accommodations.

At home, her three-year-old son, Trenton, sometimes asks her to read books that she has not yet memorized, so she has begun considering the need to learn braille. For now, however, magnifiers and a Visualtek are all she needs to read print at home and at school, since preschool materials have the advantage of big, bold, bright shapes and words.

"It's a wonderful job," she smiles. "I'm my own boss. I get to be at work all morning and at home with my child all afternoon. I love children. I just can't think of anything else I'd rather do."

SALARY: About $6,000 for nine months' teaching, after all necessary supplies are bought.

EQUIPMENT USED: *For mobility:* no adaptive devices. *For teaching preparation:* Visualtek closed-circuit television, a computer with a 17-inch (44-cm) monitor, and handheld magnifiers. No adaptive equipment at school.

ABOUT PATTY KOORS

HOME
Indianapolis, Indiana

SCHOOL
St. Thomas Aquinas

AGE
31

CAUSE OF VISUAL IMPAIRMENT
Congenital cataracts and glaucoma

VISUAL ACUITY
20/200 (6/60 [its metric equivalent]) in one eye
and 20/1000 (6/300) in the other

KINDERGARTEN TEACHER
Patty Koors

"I wanted to make school a fun place to be, so I went into teaching."

ORGANIZATION IS THE KEY to the way Patty Koors runs her classroom, her kickball team, and her life. It is also perhaps one of the main ingredients that has made her such a tremendous success in her chosen profession.

"I chose teaching for a pretty crazy reason," Koors explains. "I always hated school as a kid. And as I grew older, I loved kids. I wanted to make school a fun place to be, so I went into teaching."

Now, in her ninth year of teaching, it is clear that she has succeeded. In 1993, Koors was named Outstanding Catholic Educator of the Year in Indianapolis. She has been singled out as an Outstanding Teacher by one local television station and a Shining Star by another. And best of all, there is always a waiting list for her kindergarten.

Things did not look so splendid when Koors first graduated from Marian College in her hometown of Indianapolis 10 years ago with a bachelor's degree in education and certification to teach kindergarten through third grade. Despite her good references, honors, and high grades, prospective employers interviewed her with reservation, and she was subject to stinging remarks such as the one by a hiring supervisor who said that Koors would not get the job because he did not believe she could watch children on the playground.

After a year of substitute teaching and working part time in a Head Start program, however, her luck shifted. St. Thomas Aquinas school was about to begin a kindergarten program, and two of her respected former professors at Marian College recommended Koors.

Her students are a mix of all-day and half-day kindergartners, with a maximum of 20 students at any one time. Her teaching is hands on and in small groups, so all the children are constantly busy and she can move from table to table, keeping a close watch on every child.

"As they come in, in the morning," Koors confides, "I memorize what color each child is wearing. As the day goes on, I can't see their faces, but I know who has on a red shirt."

Does she make mistakes? "Sure," she says, "but kindergartners don't hesitate to tell you." They also do not hesitate to tattle on one another, so discipline has never been a problem.

In her classroom, every toy has its place, and all the children learn quickly that if they put a game or toy away in the wrong place or without all its pieces, they lose the use of it. That, Koors explains, may serve as an accommodation to her but is actually intended as an important lesson for the children.

Books are alphabetized on the shelf, so a chosen title is easy to find. In file cabinets, she organizes a file for every letter of the alphabet on every topic, so everything she needs can be retrieved in an instant.

When Koors reads stories aloud, the children understand that she holds the book close and directly in front of her. In other words, they can see the pictures after she has read the page, rather than during the story as they might do with a fully sighted adult. No one seems to mind.

"The kids just know that my style is routine," she says. "I teach things in a certain order. I put things away in their places."

When the children leave the room, Koors walks them in two lines, rather than one, so she can see to the end. On the playground—a conveniently walled-off area—she can see if someone has gone beyond a tree. Knowing which child it is is not always essential.

"Games and books for five-year-olds all have large print and bright colors," she says, "so I don't have much trouble seeing them." Similarly, she has no difficulty teaching children to use the three Apple computers in her classroom because "kindergarten programs are all big, bright shapes and colors, rainbows and dinosaurs, and things that are easy to see."

Koors believes that growing up in a family of seven with a mother who was blind and a father who was visually impaired undoubtedly gave her a solid foundation for the pragmatic methods that make her a successful teacher.

"We knew growing up that if we put a puzzle back without all its pieces, we couldn't have another puzzle," she says. "That was just the way it was. Everything was always organized."

Despite that background and her pride in having used recorded books through college and using a magnifier for reading print, Koors adamantly resists being identified as a visually impaired teacher. "I don't want to be thought of as a visually impaired professional or a legally blind professional," she says. "I'm just a professional."

And, indeed, that seems to be the way others view her. Only in the earliest days did parents ever question her ability to teach their children. Now, she says, her reputation proceeds her, and no questions are asked.

Koors is a frequent presenter in college classes for aspiring teachers and is deeply involved in a number of professional organizations. For several years, she has worked at every level of organizing the annual statewide conference for the Indiana chapter of the National Association for the Education of Young Children, from planning the program to chairing registration to making presentations to performing a host of other responsibilities.

On Sundays, she teaches preschool religion classes, and in warm weather, she coaches girls' kickball. "I loved the game as a kid," she says, "and didn't get to play much because everyone was so afraid I'd get hurt. Now, I coach B teams, so I can be sure everyone gets a chance."

Koors says she gets to and from school, which is about a mile (about .62 km) from her home, by bike or by riding in a car with another faculty member. For other transportation needs, she walks or takes a bus.

For decorating the classroom, her approach is to have her students do most of the work. "It's their room," she says simply. "It should be their artwork that they see around them every day. If they hang something a little crooked, who's going to care?"

For a person who chose teaching because she hated school as a child, Koors has definitely found ways of making it a wonderful place to be for some lucky kindergartners.

SALARY: $20,000–$25,000 for nine months of teaching; Koors augments her income by working at the local children's museum in the summer.

EQUIPMENT USED: *For reading and teaching preparation:* eyeglasses, a handheld magnifier, and a computer with a 20-inch (51-cm) monitor.

ABOUT MICHAEL JONES

HOME
Aptos, California

SCHOOL
Capitola Elementary School

AGE
48

CAUSE OF VISUAL IMPAIRMENT
Retinitis pigmentosa, onset in college

VISUAL ACUITY
Light perception

SECOND–THIRD-GRADE TEACHER
Michael Jones

"Never do a job a child can do."

IMAGINE A PLACE where children begin every day with a song and take trips to the beach to examine sea otters and tide pools. They play with clay and listen to spellbinding stories. They know they are important because they always have a job to do, and they know what to expect because everything has a place. Best of all, they are always learning something new.

That is life as usual for 21 seven- and eight-year-olds in Michael Jones's second–third-grade classroom in Capitola Elementary School, a public K–5 school in Aptos, in the second smallest county in California, 90 miles (145 km) south of San Francisco and just three blocks from the beach. Infusing every minute with as much energy and creativity as possible seems to be Jones's personal code for living, and his young charges for the past 19 years have reaped the benefits.

When Michael and Hibbe Jones, high school sweethearts who have been married for 27 years, first entered college, their plan was to become foreign-language teachers. The decreased foreign-language requirement for high school students and the subsequent lower demand for teachers inspired them both to change to elementary education. Hibbe shifted gears to raise their own children and now works in a rehabilitation facility for stroke survivors, and Michael became a veteran primary-grade teacher.

By his junior year in college, Jones's retinitis pigmentosa began to take a serious toll on his vision. While student teaching, he recalls, he could still write, but he could not read what he had written. He could no longer see faces and began carrying a long cane to identify himself as a visually impaired person to others. Today, he has only the slightest bit of light perception but has managed to turn his blindness into a career asset, rather than a liability.

Undaunted in the mid-1970s by the lack of offers for full-time teaching jobs, Jones took his guitar to school and landed a job teaching songs to primary-grade children.

"I knew only about 14 songs and made less money than when I'd been a custodian," he laughs, "but it got my foot in the door." When a full-time position for a second–third-grade teacher became available, Jones was hired. He has been in the same school district, Soquel Schools, for 19 years and in the same school, Capitola, since 1981. Although Jones has taught other grades, the combined second-third grade seems to be his special niche.

In a school in which every teacher is responsible for art, music, and physical education, along with the academic curriculum, Jones has traded on his strengths and personal avocations in a way that spells lively enrichment for all his students. Before he lost his sight, Jones enjoyed painting and drawing. Then he picked up the guitar and banjo to replace those creative expressions. Later, he became fascinated with clay sculpting; he now has a potter's wheel and kiln at home and at school and has begun exhibiting his pieces in local shows.

Accompanying himself and the students on the banjo or guitar, he begins each day with a song. A few times a week, in a more structured music lesson, he passes out sheets of lyrics to combine a reading lesson with the fun of making music. Some of his students can be heard on an audiocassette, *Plays Well with Others,* which Jones produced and is selling to raise funds for his classroom.

A gifted storyteller as well, Jones trades places with another teacher a few times each week to swap talents. While he tells stories and teaches music to her students, she teaches handwriting to his. ("My cursive writing wasn't good when I could see," he quips.)

Believing that children thrive with organization and structure, he says he has little difficulty with discipline because the children learn the rules from the beginning. The desks are arranged with precise symmetry, with masking tape on the floor to define individual spaces. The children take turns being "inspector"—making sure that the desks are all in place and that there is no litter on the floor. They consider it a great reward to be inspector, he says, as they do the myriad other jobs he has assigned to build skills and self-esteem.

"Never do a job a child can do" is his philosophy, believing that the more appropriate responsibility children are given, the greater will be their sense of personal worth. Every three weeks the children rotate jobs, and there are enough jobs to keep everyone happily busy. They change the calendar, empty the trash, answer the intercom, manage the playground equipment, straighten the library shelves, erase the chalkboard, and act as team captains when it is time to go outdoors.

Jones has a rule, the children know, that jackets and backpacks are to be hung on the hooks. He does not want to trip, he tells them, so the children get a double lesson: in blindness awareness and organizational habits.

Jones prepares lesson plans and weekly progress letters to parents on his home computer and brings a disk to school to print out both on a laser printer. On his classroom computer, he has games and programs for the students to play, a current favorite being a CD-ROM of the *Magic School Bus and the Rain Forest.*

The tools and techniques of blindness are casually integrated into classroom life for Jones's students. A 12-inch (31-cm) name tag taped to each child's desk at the beginning of the school year helps him identify each child's voice. The children's names are printed in large block letters for the benefit of his full-time teaching assistant, as well as in grade 1 braille. On each folder, Jones glues a braille alphabet card beneath the child's printed name. This year, as early as the second day, one girl caught an error in the brailling of her name, and Jones rewarded her with a Hershey's Kiss.

In the first week of school, Jones asks the children to bring in questions about blindness. Questions range from silly to serious: "How do you brush your teeth?" and "How do you check our work?" Jones answers each with an honest answer, sometimes having the children guess the answers first. This homework assignment stimulates conversations with their parents, Jones reasons, and the questions are uninhibited and lively. From then on, blindness takes something of a backseat. Sometimes, questions come when completely unexpected, and the teacher's sense of humor kicks into gear. He cites, for example, the time a four-year-old sibling came to open house. Jones asked the child, "So, are you in kindergarten?" "No, Mr. Jones," the child replied, "I'm over here!"

Every print book in the class library has braille on the cover, so Jones can identify it, and the computer (which everyone affectionately calls "Larry") talks, so he knows what is on the screen. Although he usually avoids writing on the chalkboard, when he does, the children can decipher what he has written and even commend him: "That's good, Mr. Jones!"

The teaching assistant generally writes on the chalkboard, in addition to helping with reading, correcting papers, and keeping the room decorated and aesthetically pleasing, among other duties. When the class walks to Monterey Bay, a national sanctuary, for some hands-on environmental learning, Jones takes along his assistant and one parent-chaperon for every five students.

Although he has taught other elementary grades, most of his teaching experience has been with third graders. They are indeed his preferred group. "They're so impressionable and cooperative at that age," he reflects. "And I enjoy getting them before the hormones kick in."

A long-distance runner, Jones enjoys running with the children for physical education, as well as teaching team sports like baseball and kickball. Since he prefers running with a guide and does not think that third graders are up to the task, he usually invites an older student to join him.

After school, Jones has been president of his local teachers' union and is involved with selecting new reading and mathematics materials for school. The motto for his lifestyle is much like his motto for keeping the students on task and interested in the classroom: Don't stand still.

SALARY: $49,000 for 10 months of teaching.

EQUIPMENT USED: *For mobility:* a long cane. *For teaching preparation:* a Pentium computer with a

DECtalk speech synthesizer and Vocal-Eyes screen-reading software, both at home and at school; an Arkenstone Open Book reading system; a Perkins Brailler; and a manual typewriter, which he still finds to be the most efficient means of dashing off a quick note to a parent or colleague.

INTERMEDIATE GRADES

ABOUT JAMES B. DUGDALE

HOME
El Monte, California

SCHOOL
Sanchez Elementary School

AGE
64

CAUSE OF VISUAL IMPAIRMENT
Retinitis pigmentosa

VISUAL ACUITY
Light perception

THIRD–FOURTH-GRADE TEACHER

James B. Dugdale

"Treat me with respect, and I'll treat you the same way."

THE 32 CHILDREN in James B. Dugdale's third–fourth-grade classroom are getting something extra mixed in with their social studies, language arts, mathematics, and science lessons. It is a generous helping of conscience training by virtue of the way their teacher has decided to handle the issue of his blindness. "You knew I couldn't see you go get a drink without permission," he tells a recalcitrant fourth grader. "That was rude." The message is simple, but it communicates clearly. "You know if you get out of your seat or pass a note, I won't see you do it," he tells his students. "But you know you're not supposed to do it, so just don't do it. Treat me with respect, and I'll treat you the same way."

Although he uses traditional methods of managing energetic elementary-age students, Dugdale depends more on his rapport with the children than on seating charts. It takes quite a while, he admits, to learn all their names, so he employs a variety of methods. Third and fourth graders are not in the same places all day, since they leave the classroom for lunch and recess and dissolve small groups for one subject to establish new ones for another. Therefore, Dugdale uses their names frequently at the beginning of the year, in an attempt to learn nuances of their voices and mannerisms that will help him remember who they are as the school year gets under way. He reminds the children to speak out with a question, rather than to raise their hands. "If you shake your heads, I won't hear them unless you've got rocks in there," he jokes. When several children have something to say, he picks one to be a caller. As that child calls another by name, he has one more opportunity to work on recognizing voices and memorizing names.

Thirteen years ago, he trained with his first dog guide, a black Labrador retriever named Harbor, who was such a popular member of the school community that an all-school assembly was held in his honor when he retired. Children from each of the classes talked about knowing Harbor and presented him with presents. The teachers presented Mr. Dugdale and Harbor with a plaque commemorating the dog's service and deserved retirement.

Both Harbor and Dugdale's current guide, yellow Lab Lynx, are pretty much just part of the decor in Dugdale's classroom. When he first brings a new dog to school, he makes a visit to every classroom, explains how the dog works for him, and invites every child to pet and say hello.

"Then I tell them, 'From now on, leave him alone!'" he chuckles. The children have a healthy respect for Dugdale's dogs as working guides, but there is always a little room for fun, too.

During class time, the dog lies in the corner (straying occasionally to lie near a student's desk) and is ready for duty when Dugdale uses him to go to lunch or to go out to supervise recess. Mostly, he says, he and his dog just stand guard, but sometimes they cannot resist getting into the action.

"I had my class out for recess while another class was having PE," he recalls, "and I just couldn't resist getting into their softball game. When I heard the ball fly, I told Harbor to go get it, and of course, the little girl got a home run and all the kids thought it was hilarious!"

As they leave school, all 500 children in school are prone to say good-bye to both Mr. Dugdale and Lynx, and it is not uncommon for them to sneak a little irresistible pat. "Every once in a while, I'll trip over somebody sitting on the floor in class," he laughs, "and I'll say, 'Hmm, what are you doing down here?,' and the student will say, 'Oh, I just wanted to pet Lynx, Mr. Dugdale.'"

Dugdale's easy way of connecting with others is not limited to his young students. Another policy is to telephone every child's parents at the beginning of the school year—just to have a conversation and establish a relationship. Later, Dugdale calls again when something significant has happened. Rather than the stereotypical bad-news calls from school, he often calls to report that a child has been especially thoughtful or cooperative that day.

When Dugdale first began teaching, his retinitis pigmentosa had progressed to the point where reading and driving were impossible, but he could still see the students' faces and the colors they were wearing. For perhaps 15 years, he has had only light perception and has had to develop additional techniques.

He listens to all the textbooks on audiocassettes and prefers to prepare his own vocabulary lists and work sheets. When students are working from reading or other textbooks in class, it is easy at this level, he says, to know by listening to them where they need help and how to help appropriately. He carries a handheld audiocassette recorder with him at all times to make notes to himself and puts braille labels on files and other items in the classroom that need to be identified.

Dugdale prepares handouts and tests on his voice-equipped computer, and the aide helps with handwriting instruction. In this, his last year of teaching before retirement, he has an aide for more than one hour per day for the first time. The second hour, he says, is being put to good use. In addition to helping with reading, writing occasional notes to parents, and correcting students' papers, the aide helps monitor the students' behavior visually, which can reinforce Dugdale's own message: "Do the right thing."

For years, one of Dugdale's after-school pastimes has been singing in three barbershop quartets for fun and fundraising. Dugdale uses his musical ability at school to trade time and talent with another fourth-grade teacher whose strong suit is teaching art. As he points out, everyone has different strengths, and it is only logical to share them.

In the mid 1980s, Dugdale was named Outstanding Teacher of the Year for his district and attended a statewide luncheon with other teachers chosen for the same honor throughout California. "When I walked out onto that stage with Harbor (who was then his dog guide) the response from that audience of my peers gave me the warmest feeling I've ever had in my life. . . . You know, you put forth an effort, you try to do a good job, but you don't know. . . . When they applauded and applauded, my peers who were chosen as the best in our field, well, I had no desire to go any further than that in recognition. It was just such a warm feeling."

Although Dugdale has been recognized by his peers as an outstanding teacher, his perspective is characteristically earthbound. "One year, my kids are all very well behaved, so I think I'm a great teacher. Another year, they're a really obstreperous bunch, so I think my teaching must be lousy," he quips.

As yet another classroom of nine- and ten-year-olds learn Dugdale's policies, it seems that the measure of his impact runs deeper than test scores. Some of these children know that their parents were Dugdale's students 30 years ago in the same school, and, like their parents, they are learning that if you treat this teacher with respect, he will respond with fairness and dignity. Blended with the necessary academic curriculum, that is a lesson well worth learning.

SALARY: $50,000 for nine months of teaching.

EQUIPMENT USED: *For mobility:* Lynx, a yellow Labrador retriever from Guide Dogs for the Blind. *For teaching preparation:* an IBM-compatible computer with Artic Business Vision and Symphonix speech synthesizer, as well as a Radio Shack hand-held audiocassette recorder.

ABOUT SANDY LAWSON

HOME
Norristown, Pennsylvania

SCHOOL
Oak Park Elementary School

AGE
50

CAUSE OF VISUAL IMPAIRMENT
Blindness due to medical error

VISUAL ACUITY
Total blindness

SIXTH-GRADE TEACHER
Sandy Lawson

"Anything at all that helps a blind teacher teach is worth it even if you only use it once or twice a year."

S ANDY LAWSON remembers the date the way some people recall birthdays, anniversaries, or the day they met a special friend. March 28, 1995: the day she woke up after open-heart surgery and knew that something else was terribly wrong.

When Lawson awoke in the recovery room, she had full awareness of her two friends and the recovery room nurse nearby. Her eyes were wide open, but it was totally black. "They thought I was going to be sick," Lawson recalls, "because I couldn't speak with the tubes in my nose and throat and I just kept pointing to my eyes. Finally, the nurse said, 'Are you blind?' And they told me later that the sheer panic filling my face told them that I was."

Although she candidly admits that "I've never been so scared in my life," Lawson never entertained the possibility of not going back to work. Except for some early forays into newspaper advertising, most of her adult life had been devoted to teaching elementary-age children, and she expected to return to teaching. Crediting her parents with instilling a strong work ethic during her childhood, her question was never *whether* to return to teaching but rather *how* to do the job without sight. For the next two school years, Lawson dedicated herself to acquiring those necessary skills.

At the Pittsburgh Guild for the Blind, Lawson learned basic techniques for living independently as a blind person. She learned to use a computer with a speech synthesizer and to travel with a long cane. Temperatures were bitter cold during her training, however—too cold for her heart, which functions at 60 percent—and she went home feeling unsure of herself and dependent.

"You can't take a person who has been sighted for almost 50 years, take all her sight, give her a cane, and expect her to just go!" Lawson says of her initial struggles with independent mobility. Just months before her triple bypass surgery, she had taught her third-grade class to spell the word *independent* and had told them, "Look at me. I am what it means to be independent." At that time, she recalls with some irony, she thought nothing of jumping into her car for an impulsive trip to Ocean City, New Jersey. She had always been single, self-sufficient, and sighted. Now, with the sudden onslaught of blindness, she felt insecure even walking out her door.

All that changed in May 1997 when she trained with her German shepherd guide, Sassy, at The Seeing Eye, Inc., in Morristown, New Jersey. "She's just the opposite of her name," Lawson says of her slower-paced, cautious canine. The following September, with Sassy at her side, she returned to her life as an educator.

Like all teachers in her suburban Philadelphia school district, she could have been assigned to any class, kindergarten through sixth grade, upon her return. To the absolute delight of Sandy Lawson and her students, however, she was assigned to the sixth grade in her former building ("on Squirrel Lane, where all the nuts teach!"), the very same children who had last been her students as third graders the year she lost her sight.

"I always thought what a special group of kids they were in third grade," she recalls, "and was devastated when I couldn't finish that year with them. We were all so attached to one another. We've had one big happy family reunion all school year, absolutely the best possible situation I could have had for coming back."

She met with all the parents at the outset of school—introducing her dog guide and demonstrating the computer with speech. The idea was to address any questions or reservations right away, but Lawson says there were absolutely no negative concerns in the group. These were parents who had known her before and recognized that she was still the same teacher, with or without her vision.

She has a full-time teaching aide who makes copies of work sheets or tests Lawson has created, corrects papers, and assists in classroom routines in whatever ways Lawson deems to be appropriate. But Sandy Lawson's teaching style has not changed a bit, she says. She still leans on her desk a great deal or sits at the computer. She continues to walk around the room while teaching—albeit now with a clear path for making her way swiftly from front to back of the classroom—but now she walks around the room with a long cane in her hand. Rather than have it be perceived as an alien object that might create distance between teacher and students, Lawson has made the cane an object of intrigue and humor. There was a guessing game going on for a week, she relates, in which she challenged students to identify the household item that was glued on the tip of her cane to prevent it from sticking in cracks and crevices. The answer? The ball from a roll-on deodorant—an ideal topic of conversation for sixth graders!

Most important, Lawson is the same teacher who left the school fully sighted in 1995—she is still relaxed and informal and still in love with her students. The only difference is that she writes less on the chalkboard. Her use of writing and drawing was once prominent, and she finds it frustrating at times now to have so much imagery in her head and to be reluctant to communicate in her previous way. She cites an example, however, of her recently drawing a claw hammer on the chalkboard to clarify a reference to the tool used for extracting nails in crates in the story "Where the Red Fern Grows." Her students got the message immediately!

A slide projector connected to her computer enables her to project images, like overhead transparencies, onto a movie screen, simply by typing at her computer keyboard. Although she does not use this particular setup often, she believes it is valuable. "Anything at all that helps a blind teacher teach," she says, "is worth it even if you only use it once or twice a year."

Lawson has had type I diabetes (insulin-dependent diabetes mellitus) for nearly 30 years (which, somewhat ironically, never affected her eyesight as it so often does in others), and the resulting neuropathy eliminated braille reading as a viable reading alternative for her. Instead, she listens to her texts on tape and develops lesson plans a week in advance on the computer. Her computer is always on in the classroom, available for quick reference to keep herself on schedule. She has a handheld audiocassette recorder with her at all times for making quick notes to herself while teaching or in faculty meetings.

In the beginning of the school year, Lawson announced that on each child's birthday, he or she could choose a friend and the two would have lunch with the teacher in the classroom. The plan escalated to the point that each day, children clamor to stay in the classroom to eat lunch with the teacher, and most days, she relents.

"I enjoy my half-hour lunch in the faculty room," she says, "but when they come up to you and say, 'Miss Lawson, this is Jeff, and Jim, Sean, Paul, and I would like to know if we could have lunch with you,' well, how can you say no? . . . We just sit at my desk, eat our lunch, and chill out. They enjoy it and I do, too."

Lawson and Sassy have made the round of the entire school, talking to all the children about dog guides and blindness. Sassy sleeps behind the teacher's desk until it is time to leave the classroom, and the students have been "well schooled in dog guide etiquette." They know, as Lawson puts it, that Sassy "is there to work, and not for their amusement."

In presenting an image of blindness to the children, Lawson takes very seriously the responsibility of shaping accurate and open attitudes. Because her own blindness resulted from medical error, she makes it a point to let children know that it was a rare instance, that she herself had been hospitalized before without incident, and that they should not be afraid it would happen to them.

Diabetes and a fragile heart take an additional physical toll on this witty, offbeat survivor, leaving little time or energy for much beyond her teaching. Still, it is the thing she loves best—and what she does exceedingly well.

SALARY: About $65,000 for nine months of teaching.

EQUIPMENT USED: *For mobility:* German shepherd guide, Sassy, from The Seeing Eye, Inc. *For teaching preparation:* IBM-compatible computer with a DECtalk speech synthesizer, JAWS for Windows 95, and an Arkenstone Open Book reading system; a slide projector connected to her computer for displaying text on a large screen; an ink-jet printer for producing class handouts or quick notes to parents; a four-track recorder for listening to texts on tape; and a handheld audiocassette recorder for personal note taking.

ABOUT MELISSA WILLIAMSON

HOME
Birmingham, Alabama

SCHOOL
East Lake United Methodist Elementary School

AGE
27

CAUSE OF VISUAL IMPAIRMENT
A birth-related virus; she lost sight in one eye at
age 18 months and in the other eye at age 6

VISUAL ACUITY
Total blindness

THIRD–SIXTH-GRADE TEACHER
Melissa Williamson

"I love kids and love learning and couldn't think of a better way to combine the two."

HIGH ENERGY and quick reaction time are two key elements of success that do not necessarily appear in the written job descriptions of teachers at East Lake United Methodist Elementary School in Birmingham, Alabama. Melissa Williamson puts it another way: "You have to keep moving," she says, by way of explaining how she, as a teacher who is totally blind, can keep track of 20 streetwise urban children all day.

When Williamson finished college five years ago, she sent résumés to 40 or 50 schools. There were plenty of interviews, but no offers. She did substitute teaching in a school for children with severe mental retardation for a while and worked as a substitute kindergarten teacher. Then the administrator of East Lake received her résumé and noticed that she and Williamson had belonged to the same college sorority.

"She's a fantastic administrator," Williamson says, "and never questioned my ability." The administrator had assumed from the beginning that Williamson would not have applied for the job if she was not competent.

In an inner-city area in which the public schools are overcrowded and violent, East Lake is attempting to offer an alternative educational environment to some parents. Providing day care for infants and a school program that runs through the sixth grade, the school is housed in the church building, and its play area is flanked on all sides by city streets. The number of students is small, and the resources are limited. The school is "multiage," combining more than one grade level in each classroom.

Williamson teaches a class of 17 children, spanning grades 3–6, and typically has the same children for a few consecutive years. She teaches a full elementary curriculum, but does so with few textbooks and plenty of hands-on examples.

After the children write in their journals each morning, Williamson has each one read with her for a brief lesson. Much of the teaching is one on one, with group activities and peer tutoring keeping others busy at all times. The school uses the whole-language method for teaching reading, immersing students in as much language as possible. Rather than texts, Williamson collects books for a pittance at yard sales and tapes a card with the title in braille inside each cover. Her classroom library now boasts about 300 books.

Science and social studies are taught in small groups, and mathematics class, she says, is a time of 100 percent chaos for her. "We teach constructivist math," she explains, "using tiles, univex cubes, anything you can actually put your hands on to teach concepts."

The room is decorated with posters, Williamson's freehand drawings, and students' artwork. Combining visual interest with history lessons, she has taped a time line around the walls of the classroom with a picture of a car at every 50 years. When the class comes across anything that occurred on the time line, she has a child make a picture of that event to add to the time line.

Low tech is the operative phrase in Williamson's approach to teaching. To teach handwriting or to see other visual concepts as drawn by her students, she uses a "screen board." This ingenious homemade adaptation consists of a heavy board with a plastic window screen placed on it. Drawing or writing produced on paper laid over the screen board can be easily interpreted by touch.

Williamson keeps an electric typewriter in the classroom to prepare individualized handouts for students and carries a slate and stylus for quick braille notes at all times.

"I don't ever sit down," Williamson says of her method of maintaining order and keeping children on task. "I am constantly walking around the classroom."

For recess outdoors, the solution is the same. "The streets are the perimeter of our play area," she explains, "and I just keep moving. There's nothing else you can do."

Despite her energy, creativity, and persistence, the reality remains that her students are mostly poor, mostly minority, and all exposed to inner-city violence. She tells of the chilling moment when she realized that children were making gang signals to one another in outdoor play and speaks matter-of-factly of those who try to trick her because she cannot see. In one of her many circuits of the classroom, she stopped to help a boy with his reading. "I reached out my hand to touch his back," she recalls, "and in his place was a giant, stuffed bunny!" Williamson responded to the incident the only way she felt she could—with a careful mix of humor and reprimand. Her bubbly, energetic personality lends itself easily to a quick laugh, even at her own expense, but she sent a clear message to the children that such tricks could never go unnoticed for very long.

Her life outside the classroom consists mostly of caring for her 18-month-old son and doing volunteer work with the National Association of Blind Educators. As a college student, she received a scholarship from the National Federation of the Blind and has since devoted hours to the federation's scholarship committee, passing along to others the same help she once received.

Her decision to teach, she says, was inspired by an outstanding teacher who worked with gifted children, including Williamson as an eighth grader. "I love kids and love learning," she says, "and couldn't think of a better way to combine the two."

After four years, Williamson says she may not stay at the same school for much longer and may take time off to raise and teach her own child. Whatever else she does, she feels she was born to be a teacher and has found the experience at East Lake to be profoundly valuable.

SALARY: $18,000 for nine months of teaching.

EQUIPMENT USED: *For mobility:* a long cane. *For teaching preparation:* at home, an IBM-compatible computer with JAWS and JAWS for Windows, a DECtalk speech synthesizer, and Arkenstone's Open Book reading system. At school, a slate and stylus and an IBM electric typewriter.

MIDDLE SCHOOL AND HIGH SCHOOL GRADES

ABOUT DAN SIMPSON

HOME
Landsdowne, Pennsylvania

SCHOOL
A variety of public and private middle and high
schools

AGE
45

CAUSE OF VISUAL IMPAIRMENT
Undiagnosed infection before birth

VISUAL ACUITY
Light perception

FREELANCE POETRY TEACHER
Dan Simpson

"When I come into a group and a kid tells me that he's just not into poetry on Monday, and then on Wednesday he's writing his own stuff and reading it to the class, then I know I'm a teacher and I love what I'm doing."

NOT EVERYONE has a clear vision of the career path ahead when they are age 19 or 20 or 21. Many find their ultimate destination by a long, circuitous path with interesting detours along the way. That has been the happy coincidence with Dan Simpson, age 45, who has just launched a brand-new career as a visiting poetry teacher.

Actually, Simpson's first aspirations involved writing and literature and teaching those pleasures to others. He fondly remembers a high school English teacher who strolled into the room wearing medieval garb and reciting English ballads. His senior year he discovered T. S. Eliot and James Joyce (particularly Joyce's *Portrait of the Artist as a Young Man*), and he was hooked on the power and beauty of language.

As a promising young musician at Pennsylvania's Muhlenberg College, however, he wound up graduating with a double major in English and music—and with a real dilemma.

"I knew that I'd love to be a college English teacher," he recalls, "but I loved playing the organ, too. I may have made my decision for the wrong reasons, but what it came down to was that lots of people could read and write poetry, but not so many could play the organ."

He went to Westminster Choir College in Princeton, New Jersey, earning a master's degree in organ performance and singing with symphonies across the United States. After his 1976 graduation, he went to Paris, France, to study with renowned French musician André Marchal, who was also blind and a significant role model.

Although his first full-time job was indeed in music (four years as organist and choir director for a church in Towson, Maryland), Simpson was ready by 1981 to try something new. Following his twin brother's example, he switched from music to computer programming. After a brief training course at The Johns Hopkins University in Baltimore, he landed a job as systems programmer with General Instrument Corporation.

Although he was with the company for nearly ten years, "the corporate sector really wasn't for me. I could make it look like I fit in, but I never really did. I wanted to write."

After a careful study of university writing programs, Simpson left his job and enrolled in a master's program at Pennsylvania State University. There, he took his time, studying with writers he admired and allowing ample time for his own artistic talent as poet to flourish. Eventually, the old idea of teaching was rejuvenated.

A friend suggested that he take a methods course, just to have some teaching basics, and from there he wound up in pursuit of a student teaching opportunity.

"I couldn't go just anywhere for my student teaching," he muses. "We had to find a teacher at a school where they could see the challenge of taking a blind guy in his forties with a ponytail, and say, 'hey, this looks exciting, let's take it on.'" At Central High School, a magnet school in Philadelphia, Mickey Harris was just such a teacher.

For the duration of the 1996–97 school year, Simpson did his student teaching with Harris—and became enchanted with the process of teaching teenagers to read and write poetry.

Since then, he has been busily developing a niche for himself as a freelance poetry teacher, teaching a week or more at a time in various private and public middle schools and high schools. At the Torah Academy in Philadelphia, for example, he was first commissioned to teach poetry to boys for one week. Then a week of teaching the girls was added to his contract and, finally, yet a third week of teaching a coed group in the school's junior high.

Each school is different, and the intimacy with individual students that he enjoyed over a yearlong teacher-student relationship at Central is missing, but Simpson says he loves the freedom his current life affords. "Classroom teachers often feel inadequate to teach poetry," he comments, "because they have so much else to do. I come in and concentrate on poetry alone, and I know I'm doing something important."

He works from braille texts whenever possible and notes made from tapes when braille is not available. He creates his own handouts—poems, discussion questions, guidelines for writing assignments—on his IBM-compatible computer at home. On his Reading Edge reading machine, he scans printed texts to be used in class, then prints them out in braille with his Braille Blazer embosser.

The only equipment he typically carries into classes is his Braille 'n Speak and a slate and stylus. He asks for student volunteers whenever possible—as a way of keeping them involved and getting to know them better. He asks a student, for instance, to write questions from his dictation on the chalkboard. He asks students to give him a guided tour of the school buildings (which, he says, are sometimes more descriptive than orientation he has received from professional mobility instructors). When he shows films in class that relate to literary topics being discussed, he asks individual students to sit beside him and describe parts in the films that are presented only visually so that they can help him obtain information that is already available to them as sighted viewers.

Working from songs by Leonard Cohen or poems by Gary Sotto, Simpson manages to extract insightful observations from students others might think too immature to understand poetry. Once, he says, he took one of his own poems into an eighth-grade class and asked the students to help him revise it.

"There's a problem in this poem and I wondered if you could help me fix it," he told them, and was astonished at the conversation that ensued. "They didn't even have the poem in front of them," he recalls, explaining that he had simply read it to them from his braille copy. "And they were moving lines around, suggesting alternative images—having the kind of conversations that a college class of writers might have."

Although he was frequently alone with his classes during the period of student teaching, Simpson says that as a visiting poet he now asks that a classroom teacher remain in the room. Because of the limited time he has with each school, he says it is just simpler and a time-saving measure to eliminate any potential discipline problems by having the full-time teacher present.

Simpson travels to classes with his yellow Labrador guide, Yaeger, often using trains, subways, and buses to get to and from his students. In the classroom, Yaeger typically lies beside the teacher's desk, leaving Simpson to move freely among the students. With desks arranged in a U shape, he feels he is never more than a few steps from any individual.

"When I come into a group and a kid tells me that he's just not into poetry on Monday, and then on Wednesday he's writing his own stuff and reading it to the class," Simpson reflects, "then I know I'm a teacher and I love what I'm doing."

His goal is to find the balance between teaching and writing that will not compromise his own time as poet. Striving to find that balance and survive financially, Simpson believes he may have found the career where he truly belongs.

SALARY: About $600 per week.

EQUIPMENT USED: *For mobility:* Yaeger, a yellow Labrador guide from Guiding Eyes for the Blind. *For teaching preparation:* IBM-compatible computer with Artic Business Vision software and a Symphonix synthesizer; a Reading Edge reading machine; a DeskJet printer; a Braille Blazer embosser; a Perkins Brailler; and various audiocassette recorders. When teaching, he usually carries only a Braille 'n Speak and a slate and stylus.

ABOUT FRANK LOPEZ

HOME
Sacramento, California

SCHOOL
C. K. McClatchy High School

AGE
47

CAUSE OF VISUAL IMPAIRMENT
Progressive nuclear ophthalmoplegia

VISUAL ACUITY
Total blindness

AUTOMOTIVE AND DIESEL TECHNOLOGY TEACHER

Frank Lopez

"When they think they're just helping me by reading a gauge, they're actually learning."

PEOPLE WHO KNOW Frank Lopez know that they do not have to look much further for living proof of the power of self-determination and believing in one's own capabilities. In 1989, Frank Lopez lost his sight and lost his job. His family lived on food stamps and disability income. But he never stopped moving forward.

Even before he became totally blind, Lopez's choice of work was a bit unconventional. Diagnosed as legally blind since childhood, Lopez spent the first 17 years of his adult work life maintaining and repairing diesel engines that kept Los Angeles fire fighters, paramedics, and other emergency personnel on the job. For 17 years, that hands-on work was a viable means of supporting his family. Then the pinpoint of visual field he depended on vanished, and it was time to reevaluate his career options.

Losing his job and subsequently his home were no small blows, but they never daunted the Lopez self-esteem or capacity for creative solutions. He went to the vocational rehabilitation system in California with a sound suggestion for his future.

"I've been working on cars and tearing apart engines all my life," he told his counselor. "I'd like to go back to college so I can teach those skills to others."

He can laugh now about the employment evaluation that suggested he assemble ballpoint pens in a Goodwill workshop. Eventually, though, he found funding and support to go back to college for teaching credentials.

Lopez credits his wife, Judy, and their cemented relationship for getting him through the rocky transition. With four young children at the time, they drove 70 miles (113 km) each way to and from his college courses. Sometimes Judy sat in class along with her husband, taking notes. Other times she wandered off to the library or elsewhere to pursue her own interests.

Getting a job was no easier than initially convincing others that he could teach auto mechanics had been. Lopez never gave up on himself, though, and never hesitated to go the extra mile to convince a potential employer that he was fully capable of teaching high school students how to repair and maintain engines. Asked on an application about physical impairment, Lopez noted that he was "a qualified visually impaired person who could do the job." Once in an interview, he greeted the silent discomfort of potential employers by opening the subject of how he, as a blind person, was able to teach teens to repair engines and able to do the job himself.

He volunteered in one high school for an entire year, taking over the class as substitute when the regular teacher was not there and showing up day in and day out to lend a hand. He was recognized for that effort and believes that every effort led to his ultimately finding the teaching job he now holds.

When Judy Lopez noticed a job announcement that perfectly fit her husband's qualifications, the couple was not discouraged by the fact that it was located in Sacramento, 500 miles (806 km) north of where they were currently living.

"I didn't have money for a plane ticket or a suit to wear to the interview," Lopez recalls, "so I went to rehab again and they paid for both."

The Lopez family, now with six children, relocated two days before Lopez first reported for work. Presently in his fourth year of teaching, Lopez has attracted much local recognition—from newspaper features to a five-minute spot in a local TV evening news broadcast. Parents are thrilled to meet the celebrity teacher, and students have nothing but respect for the teacher who—with amazing accuracy and great sense of humor—works magic on any engine.

At McClatchy High School, Lopez has found his career niche. He moves from car to car in the modern facility adjacent to his classroom, listening to an engine here, helping students locate a problem there, moving, joking, and encouraging.

"I tell them I can do this with my eyes closed," he laughs, "so they certainly can, too!"

As a child with limited vision in the Los Angeles school system, Lopez says he was fortunate in that "they groomed me to be blind." Even though he was able to read large-print materials then, he was taught braille and other adaptive techniques. When he actually became totally blind in 1989, his training was more a brushup than a crash course, and he believes that condition made his transition much smoother.

Although he knows the braille code well, years of working on engines have taken their toll in the form of carpal tunnel syndrome and a numbness in one hand. He reads personal notes with his right hand only, he says, and now finds long sessions at the computer difficult. Still, his Braille 'n Speak and Perkins Brailler are vital support tools to his teaching, as are tape recorders and his Kurzweil Personal Reader for scanning printed materials. After a recent computer evaluation, it was recommended that a software package called Voila be obtained for him, which would enable him to use Dragon Dictate and JAWS for Windows (thus having both voice input and output capabilities) simultaneously. Because his school recently purchased laptop computers for all other faculty members, his hope is that one with the recommended software will soon be purchased for him as well.

Lopez also has some specially adapted instruments—a talking micrometer (to measure with thousandths of an inch) and a talking tachometer (for announcing that an idle is, say, 750 RPMs)—but chooses not to use them at school. It is much more effective to teach the students to use such instruments, he believes, if they have to "help" the teacher a bit by reading them. "When they think they're just helping me by reading a gauge," he says, "they're actually learning."

A full-time teaching aide assists with such visual details as confirming that students are wearing eye protection, correcting papers, or providing Lopez with verbal cues from his sometimes nonverbal students. Some of the students have developmental disabilities and some are not proficient in English, which can lead to a minimum of auditory feedback. "She had to tell me that I was speaking too fast in lecture," he cites an example of the aide's support, "and that I needed to allow time for them to reflect a bit. Now I remind myself to slow down."

But no one can do the actual hands-on teaching but Lopez himself. When one student told the teacher about his mother's car "hopping" each time it was dropped into gear, Lopez told him to bring it in for a look. The minute Lopez sat behind the wheel and started the engine, he heard the problem. "I told the students to pop open the hood and take a look at the motor mounts. They were broken. They bought the parts and fixed the car."

Lopez jokes that he can start the cars and fix them, but he does not test drive. His own family vehicle is good testimony to his ability. He always has maintained and repaired the cars driving the eight Lopezes around but cannot remember doing more than oil changes on their 1990 Chevy Suburban since he rebuilt the transmission some years ago.

The high percentage of students with disabilities entering the automotive program inspired Lopez to return to school. In 1997, he enrolled in a master's degree program at California State University at Sacramento, where he hopes to write his thesis on the operation of a program, pending approval. "I wrote a proposal," he explains, "to operate the shop like a small business to teach some essential life skills to my students with disabilities. Teachers and parents would bring in their cars for repair, and we'd have to purchase parts, keep inventory, run a billing operation" and, of course, repair the automobiles!

Life for the Lopez family has dramatically improved since those days in 1989 when they lived in subsidized housing and on food stamps. Lopez attributes the success to the bond of love in his marriage and in his family. Today, settled into their five-bedroom Sacramento home, the Lopez family is as lively as one might expect with six children ranging in age from 5 to 16. Now that he is both teaching full time and back in graduate school himself, Lopez concedes that he has little time for much beyond work, school, and simply enjoying his children.

His older children remember him as sighted, whereas his five-year-old twin daughters have only known their daddy as a blind person. While his 14-year-old son makes jokes—"Dad, if you were legally blind before, does that mean you're illegally blind now?"—his five-year-old twins think that every daddy should have a reading machine! "They love to hear the Kurzweil read *Goodnight Moon* and such stories," Lopez laughs, "and they can't imagine that not every daddy has a machine like that."

Clearly, this attitude of acceptance and love comes from the one they have learned from their parents, and it seems to be the same one that dominates Lopez's classes at school. Even though he always carries his long cane, Lopez says there are students who will test to see if he really is blind. When he walked into a colleague's classroom to borrow something, a student who had not been in one of Lopez's classes told her teacher, "He's not blind. He walked right up to your desk. The rumor is that he's a narc on campus, here to bust kids with drugs."

Lopez gets a kick out of the story—as he gets a kick out of everything. He talks fast, works hard, loves his job and his family, and, as he puts it, "If I can wave the banner a little bit to let people know that a blind person can do something that isn't a traditional job, well, then, I'm going to take that opportunity."

SALARY: About $40,000 for nine months of teaching.

EQUIPMENT USED: *For mobility:* a long cane. *For teaching preparation:* Braille 'n Speak; a Perkins Brailler; a Dymo braille labeler; talking micrometers and other tools (but he rarely uses them at school); various audio-cassette recorders; and a Kurzweil Personal Reader.

ABOUT TARI LIVINGSTON-HUGHES

HOME
Los Angeles, California

SCHOOL
John F. Kennedy Senior High School

AGE
44

CAUSE OF VISUAL IMPAIRMENT
Retinopathy of prematurity (related to premature birth)

VISUAL ACUITY
Total blindness

ENGLISH TEACHER
Tari Livingston-Hughes

"I don't know what else I'd do."

THE ROAD to becoming a teacher may have begun with a childhood dream, but getting there was far from a fairytale for Tari Livingston-Hughes. Livingston-Hughes clearly recalls the day in kindergarten when she announced to her mother that she would be a teacher when she grew up. After 19 years as a high school English teacher for the Los Angeles Unified School District, she also still clearly recalls the difficulty she had completing the necessary steps to becoming a certified teacher.

It was the 1970s, and the Department of Education at Westmont College in Santa Barbara, California, was simply not prepared to encourage its only blind student. When Livingston-Hughes was finally given a student teaching assignment, it was the weekend before school started. She was assigned to four different master teachers in four different classrooms and given no time to obtain material in braille or another accessible format. "I was set up to fail," she says, "and that's what I did."

Still, she did not give up her dream of teaching. After taking a year off to reexamine her goals and strategies for achieving them, she enrolled in California State University at Northridge. Initially, she says, "they didn't want me either, but when they saw a grade-point average of 3.87, they began thinking that perhaps I had something to offer."

After 12 additional credits of English composition, literary criticism, grammar, and the history of English, as well as some repetition of teaching methods courses, Livingston-Hughes was ready for student teaching. She was assigned to a "master teacher" who, she says, has been her "guiding star" for 20 years and from whom she finally received the acceptance, encouragement, and mentoring every aspiring teacher needs to get up and running.

Her master teacher believed that 10th-grade English would be the best place for Livingston-Hughes to begin, and, indeed, that is where she has spent most of her 19 years of teaching. When the Los Angeles Unified School District initially telephoned to hire her, she recalls, she thought the call was for an interview. Only when she arrived at the school did she realize that the summons had been to start working.

At John F. Kennedy Senior High School, Livingston-Hughes teaches four sections of tenth-grade English and an additional course called Books for Pleasure, which is designed to encourage reading among nonacademic seniors. She loves her job, does it well, and has masterfully assembled an arsenal of equipment and interpersonal skills to achieve success.

A braille user since early childhood, Livingston-Hughes prefers to have copies of works she is teaching in braille. Since the earthquake on January 17, 1994, however, it has simply not been possible to do so. An entire building on her school's campus was destroyed in that earthquake—and all her braille books in her classroom. Many of the braille books were too old to be replaced.

When brailled copies are not available, she uses audiotaped copies of books or an Optacon to check page numbers and a phrase or two. Of all the equipment in her classroom, it is the Optacon that she finds the most indispensable. "I use the Optacon to check just about everything, like xerox copies before handing them out, to read a book title on the shelf, or to keep my place while we are reading," she explains.

Other standard pieces of equipment in her classroom are the Keynote XL laptop computer; the Reading Edge reading machine; the Perkins Brailler; and either an audiocassette recorder or the Combination Machine, issued for reading specially recorded materials by the National Library Service (NLS) for the Blind and Physically Handicapped.

With the Keynote computer, she creates new files each semester for class lists, records of grades, and lists of everything each student has done for class. Although she uses a standard computer printer for producing directions for students, tests, and so on, the Keynote's "microprinter" has been the only solution she has found to respond quickly when a student "needs a note right now." This built-in printer enables the user to create and print notes instantly, on three-inch-wide (about 8-cm-wide) paper—a convenient method and perfect size for a quick excuse to be out of class or a message to a parent.

Livingston-Hughes records daily attendance in braille on file cards and keeps track of all work turned in by the students. She has found it much more efficient, however, for her assistant to maintain the physical grade books, so that all "legal aspects of the job are readily available in print form to anyone who would need to see them."

By California law, a blind teacher is allowed to have a full-time classroom assistant, when needed, and an additional 15 hours of reading assistance. Livingston-Hughes's assistant keeps the legally required teaching records, helps manage the classroom, organizes the students' materials, reads school-related mail, and sometimes directs oral reading sessions.

The assistants have come from all walks of life. Some have been college students, some have been parents returning to college, and some have been retirees. All have been required by law to take at least 12 college units per year.

Although Livingston-Hughes concedes that her 19 years of teaching have not been without pitfalls, she has applied a healthy blend of practical techniques and common sense to solve them all. Sure, she says, students will try to call out for an absent friend during roll call, but either she or her assistant has always caught the offense. Sure, the chaos of losing her classroom and braille books to an earthquake presented challenges, but she faced them one day at a time, along with her colleagues.

Still, teaching the 10th grade is what she hopes to continue doing. "Most of my students are Latino," she comments, "so they often have not had the same richness of experience with language that many of us have had. . . . You don't just throw a story at them. . . . You build a bridge of what they need to know and help them understand what they are reading aloud to one another."

Getting to and from school involves an 80-minute ride on two buses, but Livingston-Hughes prefers this solution to depending on others for car transportation. Whether this preference arises from an overall style of centering her life on order and detail or whether depending on herself more than others is a natural outgrowth of an adult life of singlehood is anybody's guess. (The hyphenated name is not, as often is assumed, two names hyphenated in marriage; rather, as she puts it, "I was born hyphenated.") Despite the long commute and full teaching schedule, she finds time to serve on a variety of school committees; attend educators' conferences; sing in her church choir; be involved with several radio clubs; and participate in Daughters of the King, a worldwide organization of women involving, among other things, community service and daily prayer.

Asked how she feels about fulfilling her dream as a kindergartner of growing up to be a teacher, she says simply, "I don't know what else I'd do."

SALARY: After 19 years, $50,000 for a nine-month school year; an additional $5,000 for teaching summer school.

EQUIPMENT USED: *For mobility:* a "flock of canes." *For teaching preparation:* the Reading Edge reading machine, Optacon, Keynote XL laptop computer, a printer and microprinter, the Perkins Brailler, an NLS-compatible audiocassette recorder, and a Combination Machine.

ABOUT GARY LEGATES

HOME
Westminster, Maryland

SCHOOL
Westminster High School

AGE
46

CAUSE OF VISUAL IMPAIRMENT
Retinopathy of prematurity (related to premature birth)

VISUAL ACUITY
Total blindness

LATIN AND FRENCH TEACHER
Gary LeGates

"There's a rumor that [I] can catch paper airplanes."

E ven though his grade-point average at Western Maryland College was a 3.5 and his student teaching was rated A, Gary LeGates found that no one wanted to hire a blind Latin teacher when he entered the job market over 20 years ago. Like so many students, his solution initially was to arm himself with more education.

LeGates applied for and was offered a graduate assistantship at Pennsylvania State University, where he taught Latin to first-year college students and earned a master's degree in classics. He returned home to Westminster to a flurry of interviews, but no school, not even in his hometown school district, was hiring a blind Latin teacher.

LeGates and his vocational rehabilitation counselor then planned to enroll him in the Randolph-Sheppard vending program, with the understanding that if he was offered a teaching job, he would leave that program. However, things never had to go that far.

When LeGates learned that the Latin teacher at Westminster High School would be going on maternity leave, he called the chair of the foreign language department to see if the job would be available. When the principal asked the department chair for recommendations, the department chair named LeGates, who had done a stellar job for her as a student teacher. The principal also knew his work and called to offer him the job. LeGates believes, however, that the recommendation from the department chair was the single factor that landed him the offer. Although he got the job because of another teacher's maternity leave, LeGates says he was never treated as a substitute, but rather as a full-time teacher from the outset. When the other teacher returned to work a year later, she was assigned to another school. LeGates has taught in the same high school since 1977.

LeGates is a full-time Latin teacher and a half-time French teacher, which means that he teaches all four years of Latin and an occasional French I or II class. He acts as an adviser to the high school's Latin Club, is a coadviser to the French Club, and has been integral in writing curricula for Latin programs throughout Carroll County, Maryland.

He works entirely from brailled texts, prepared by the National Braille Association. At times, he stands at the front of the room at a podium, teaching directly from the text. At other times, he walks around the room, working with students in small groups or just circulating to listen more closely to individual students or rows. Since the 1995 addition of the Proxima machine to his collection of teaching tools, he also teaches from the back of the room.

With the Proxima, LeGates can type on his laptop computer and display the text on an overhead projector at the front. This piece of technology has been a tremendous breakthrough for any teacher, but particularly for a blind teacher who finds it difficult to write on a chalkboard. With the Proxima, LeGates says, the aspects of communicating with students visually can be much more spontaneous.

In addition to the Proxima, LeGates has recently begun making his own transparencies with a computer and laser printer. This method works very well. With the exception of the Proxima, LeGates always has purchased all his own equipment. "I know there's a lot of debate about that sort of thing," he says, "but my attitude has always been that they didn't hire someone to eat up the school's money. They hired a teacher. And they wouldn't buy a sighted teacher a car."

LeGates has never had an aide or assistant in the classroom and, until just a few years ago, always paid for his own readers. For tests, he recruits volunteers from his church or elsewhere to come into the classroom as monitors. For short quizzes, he sometimes drafts a hall monitor to act as a sighted backup.

"There's no doubt that even a tiny bit of sight would make teaching 50 percent easier," LeGates says in honest appraisal of the challenges to a blind high school teacher. "With just a small amount of sight, you could see when a student was laying a paper on your desk or doing something he or she shouldn't do. You could write on the chalkboard, or be more useful in such areas as cafeteria duty or parking lot duty." Yet, with no sight, he has found creative solutions to paperwork challenges and to the dilemma of discipline. When he finds a paper on his desk, he immediately places it in his folder to be examined later by a reader. Maybe it is nothing significant at all, but the habit guarantees that he remains in control of the situation.

As for not having any sight in regard to behavioral issues, he has combined creativity and just plain good luck to his advantage. Once, in a homeroom that was populated by particularly difficult students (most of whom had been arrested), a student threw a paper airplane that just happened to sail right into his hand. It was serendipity, but now, he says, "there's a rumor that LeGates can catch paper airplanes."

Homeroom, however, is no longer a problem. The primary function of homeroom was to take attendance and process "a ton of paperwork" at the beginning of the year. Emergency cards, attendance forms, and other pieces of paper needed to be completed on every student, and behavior was a problem. The homeroom students were not the ones LeGates would be teaching. After five or six years, he asked for an alternate duty and was able to trade early-morning office duty for the homeroom stint.

In the office, he answers the telephone, takes messages for teachers, and writes down the details of phoned-in absences. He used to bring along his manual typewriter (which he still keeps in his classroom for typing a quick note now and then) but now uses the office computer.

Although discipline did not figure into his choice of a specialty, LeGates now believes that in terms of coping with disciplinary problems, he could not have chosen a better subject to teach. "Kids who take Latin are generally well-behaved kids," he observes. "They have goals. They want to learn."

He depends extensively on computers, both at home and at school, to do his job. He keeps grades on the computer in WordPerfect files and then prints them out on braille paper to compute them. He prepares all classroom handouts and tests in WordPerfect and prints them on a laser printer.

LeGates has good rapport with his students, who see him as fair but strict, and talks openly about his blindness "when it comes up." He tries to take one period each semester for open questions about blindness and adaptive techniques and chuckles that his students know it is a good way to get him off the subject of Latin.

On field trips over the years—to art museums and Roman-style restaurants—students have always been naturally accommodating, and LeGates admits that although such trips make him apprehensive, they have always gone extremely well. He has held picnics for the Latin Club at his home and laughs at the memory of once overhearing a student say to another, "I wondered what this place would look like." The curiosity, he says, when the students learn that both he and his wife are blind, is perfectly natural and generally dissipates when they discover that there is nothing extraordinary about the way he lives.

In a school of about 2,000 students, the sizes of LeGates's Latin I through Latin IV classes have continued to range from 9 to 35 students. Even when Latin is not fashionable, he says, "kids hang in there because they like the teacher."

Besides advising the Latin and French clubs and writing curricula for Latin teachers throughout the county, LeGates has a rich extracurricular life. He is a deacon of his church, has been president of the Maryland School for the Blind's Alumni Association, and is first vice president of the National Association of Blind Teachers.

Along with impressive successes, LeGates does not hesitate to admit to disasters. "The worst thing that ever happened in the classroom," he recalls, "was when my windows were open, and a lawn mower outside made it impossible for me to hear anything. A kid climbed out the window, stole ice cream from a nearby ice cream truck, and brought it back to class." More than half the students reported the infraction.

To balance that one incident, however, are the years of good evaluations and students who write him or return to visit. And there were students who worked frantically on special projects just because they liked their teacher, not knowing they would get extra credit.

In 1997, LeGates was named one of the 10 most distinguished teachers in Carroll County, just one of the many teaching awards for which he has been nominated or selected. In a nomination letter for that honor, the chair of his department wrote that he "inspires many students to learn and to build confidence by his example." In any language, that statement translates into achievement worthy of genuine pride.

SALARY: $45,000 for nine months of teaching.

EQUIPMENT USED: *For mobility:* a long cane. *For teaching preparation:* a Proxima; a computer with Artic Transport, Artic Business Vision, and Artic WinVision for speech access to DOS and Windows; a Toshiba laptop computer; a Romeo braille printer; a laser printer; an Omni 1000 for reading; Braille 'n Speak; a Perkins Brailler; an audiocassette recorder; and a Smith Corona manual typewriter.

ABOUT DON THORNTON

HOME
Moore, Oklahoma

SCHOOL
Moore High School

AGE
43

CAUSE OF VISUAL IMPAIRMENT
Retinitis pigmentosa

VISUAL ACUITY
Light perception

SCIENCE TEACHER
Don Thornton

"I love the teaching."

I T COULD BE ARGUED that Don Thornton became a science teacher because of his visual impairment. Looking back at his college career and the selection of majors, Thornton jokes that he had about 30 majors, including pharmacy and chemistry, before he focused on laboratory technology and earned his bachelor of science degree. He did not set out to teach. Rather, "they offered me a job and I took it."

Something must have been right about that offer, however, because 17 years later, Thornton is still teaching high school sciences in the same school that first hired him. Today, with the wisdom of hindsight, he realizes that the disease that played havoc with his visual acuity also had something to do with his difficulty identifying his areas of strength.

His visual acuity was only 20/400 (6/120 [its metric equivalent]) in both eyes when he began teaching, but he continued to pretend that he could see. All his time outside school hours was spent preparing for class because reading was such an arduous task and pretending to see when he could not was exhausting.

Finally, in the late 1980s, Thornton realized that he could no longer hide his blindness. "I couldn't read any print," he recalls, "and I couldn't see faces. I later learned that other teachers had been quietly running interference in the halls for me for some time, directing kids out of the way so I wouldn't run into them. But I thought nobody knew."

The bad news was that once he defined himself as a blind person, the school administrators defined him as an incompetent. If he could not see, they reasoned, then he could not teach. Parents, retired teachers, and former students were all willing to serve as classroom aides, and lawyers in nearby Oklahoma City wrote letters of support. Luckily, the crisis passed without a lawsuit, and money was found in the school budget to hire an aide.

The same aide has been with Thornton for eight years now—assisting in classroom management, correcting papers, and performing other strictly visual aspects of the job. "She's not there for the kids or to teach," he states simply; "she's there for me."

Although his teaching methods did not change radically, Thornton acquired some new techniques with his acceptance of blindness that relieved some of the burden of what he now calls his former denial. He learned to use a long cane, practicing its techniques night after night in his familiar neighborhood. He learned the braille alphabet to label files and equipment in his classroom. Perhaps most significant, he began using a computer equipped with a speech synthesizer and optical character recognition software, so he can now read and write the necessary teaching materials without assistance.

None of it was easy. Never having learned to type, Thornton went to the public library and checked out a typing tutorial that included an audiocassette that identified the location of the keys. With his screen-reading program for feedback, he learned when he was pressing the proper keys on the keyboard. With persistence, he managed to obtain the science texts on computer disk from the textbook publishers and now makes up most of his own tests and answer keys on the computer.

Although Thornton has taught chemistry, anatomy, and other sciences in the past, his current specialty is biology. He teaches three sections of General Biology and two sections of Basic Biology, a scaled-down version of the same subject matter designed for students with learning problems.

His classes are a blend of lecture and laboratory, depending on the time of year and the particular group of students. In the beginning of the year, for example, students have labs two or three times per week while studying cells and learning to use microscopes. In other units, there may be more lecture than lab time in class.

His teaching style is a creative combination of lecture, interaction, and hands-on teaching. When a student has trouble dissecting an earthworm, frog, or rat, the only way to understand the situation is to touch and establish clear verbal communication. He finds both to be effective, although never easy. Sometimes, he says, a student will be reluctant to ask his help, assuming that a problem is too visual for him to comprehend.

"One student couldn't see anything under the microscope," he cites an example, "and at first she didn't want to talk to me about it. I explained to her that most things work according to certain principles, and you don't need to see them to understand. I adjusted the focus and discovered that she didn't have the lens snapped into place. Finally, she said, 'I see something!'" And more than one lesson had been learned.

Thornton develops permanent seating charts for his classes and then memorizes them. He calls on students frequently, placing a high value on learning their individual characteristics and voices as early as possible. The first week, he talks about blindness with new students. He tells them, for example, to keep their feet and purses out of the aisles and to "do one of two things when you see me in the hall: Either say 'Hello, Mr. Thornton, this is so-and-so,' so I know who you are. Or run like heck to get out of my way!"

His experience has proved that once the initial curiosity about blindness is satisfied, the topic rarely comes up. Still, he reminds his students to identify themselves when speaking, both in and out of class, and does not hesitate to use his own difficulties as a benchmark for encouraging them.

When students complain, for instance, that the reading assignment is too hard to complete, Thornton tells them that if he can do it, they can do it. When they say his tests are difficult, he shows them exactly how he makes one up and invites them to do so themselves. Although it does not alter his reputation as a hard teacher, the exercise generally shows students that their own test questions are similar to his.

Outside school, Thornton can be found toiling in his flower gardens, building a gazebo, or playing beep ball or golf. After so many years of struggling over print, he now devours books on tape and has one going whenever possible. "The librarian couldn't understand why my Talking-Books machine was so dirty," he laughs, "but it had gone into the garden with me."

He also spends a fair amount of time cheering students at their sports events or welcoming graduates who drop by for a chat. "I love the teaching," Thornton says. But he adds with real candor, "it's the baby-sitting that can be discouraging." When students do not want to be there and do not want to learn, Thornton says, his job takes far more energy than when students are actively interested in what he can show them.

"There are some real problems in public schools," he cautions, "and the work can be mentally taxing." Still, if public school is where one is, Thornton has firm notions of how best to cope.

Telephoning parents often is an established habit he takes very seriously—and not just to report bad news. Sometimes he calls just to tell parents how hard their son or daughter is trying or what an upbeat young person they are sending to school. "It's so common to hear parents say that no one ever called with good news," he says, "and it's so important to do that."

A bonus in calling parents is that word gets around, and students who may cause trouble are a bit less likely to do so when they know that Thornton will inform their parents. The link between home and school, in other words, is more believable.

Teaching biology provides moments of inspiration and humor, too. It is always a pleasure to see a girl who thought she was squeamish become totally involved in dissection or a "kid who can't keep his mouth shut get squirted!"

SALARY: About $32,000 for nine months' teaching.

EQUIPMENT USED: *For mobility:* a long cane. *For teaching preparation:* a computer with a Vocal-Eyes screen reader and a Multivoice speech synthesizer, an Arkenstone Open Book reading system, and Grade Guide software for tabulating and printing out grades.

COLLEGE

ABOUT LAWRENCE W. BAGGETT

HOME
Boulder, Colorado

SCHOOL
University of Colorado

AGE
58

CAUSE OF VISUAL IMPAIRMENT
Severe injury at age five

VISUAL ACUITY
Total blindness

PROFESSOR OF MATHEMATICS
Lawrence W. Baggett

"The academic life is a good life. You are with bright, interesting people. The work is always different and new."

"THERE ARE STILL two difficult things about teaching," says Lawrence W. Baggett, a professor of mathematics at the University of Colorado. Then dropping for a moment into a mock drawl, which may be a remnant of his Mississippi babyhood, he says, "They're readin' and writin', and I have yet to solve either of those problems to my satisfaction."

It is perhaps a blend of humility, humor, and an honest appraisal of difficulty that have led to Baggett's 31 years of success in his chosen career. In any event, the success and job satisfaction are readily apparent even in a brief conversation with him, as is the personal warmth that must reassure class after class of advanced mathematics students.

Totally blind since age five, Baggett says he was lucky to have received his earliest training at the Perkins School for the Blind in Watertown, Massachusetts, where his parents happened to be living after they left Mississippi. When he was in the third grade, his family moved again to Florida, where he was enrolled briefly in the Florida School for the Blind in St. Augustine.

It was shortly after World War II, and "the school was still pretty much a broom-making and chair-caning outfit," Baggett recalls. For him that was not a happy situation. His parents knew something of the value of education and somehow persuaded the staff of a small public school nearby to accept their blind child as a student.

Baggett did not think about majoring in mathematics until his junior year at Davidson College in North Carolina, when he realized how many mathematics credits he had. From then on, mathematics was his chosen field—through a master of science degree and a doctorate in mathematics, both earned at the University of Washington in Seattle.

Although Baggett recognizes that mathematics is a field with relatively few blind people, he believes it offers some real advantages. Much of the work is done in your head, he says, and there is not the voluminous amount of reading that is required in some other fields.

Since 1966, he has taught a whole spectrum of mathematics courses—from "simple" ones like algebra to advanced courses, such as calculus, probability, and functional analysis—at the University of Colorado. Because he teaches primarily advanced graduate-level classes, the classes are small, from 10 to 16 students, thus minimizing the obstacles of "readin' and writin'" significantly.

Although he has used computers on the job since 1983—first using a tape-based VersaBraille to gain access to the university's mainframe computer, and eventually using personal computers to prepare his own class material—Baggett believes that technology has enabled him to be much more independent in his work than he could have been without it. A software package called TEX, widely used by people in the mathematics field, enables him to type such words as *alpha, integral,* or *degree* and have the corresponding Greek letters or mathematics symbols appear in the final product.

When he taught larger classes, Baggett used a graduate student to read homework papers to him. With smaller advanced classes, however, he now has each student report homework to him individually. This more casual, personal approach not only eliminates the need for reading assistance but enables him to become better acquainted with all the students and to provide more individualized attention to each one.

To prepare lectures, he has used a combination of recorded books; books on computer disks (which he has had some success obtaining from textbook publishers); and, in the case of his functional analysis course, working from the textbook he wrote that is widely used by other mathematics professors as well.

Teaching, research, and service are the three components of an academic career, and Baggett has excelled in each. In addition to the functional analysis textbook, he has published dozens of articles in mathematics journals and has presented papers at mathematics conferences. He has also served on numerous committees over the years and was chair of the mathematics department for three years. Currently, he administers the University Math Program, a self-paced collection of precalculus courses taken by thousands of students. For credits in such courses as algebra and trigonometry, students work from videotaped lectures and monitor their own progress. Baggett manages the budget, equipment, and course materials that keep the program going.

His teaching load is typically two courses per semester—harmonic analysis and wavelet theory at this writing, for instance—and the class sizes are small. Communicating concepts in class would generally involve writing on the chalkboard, but Baggett says he only occasionally resorts to this teaching technique. "Because I lost my sight at such an early age," he explains, "handwriting has never come naturally to me. Some of my students have learned to decipher my scratches on the board, but I try to communicate as much as I can verbally." Because the level of mathematics he teaches is more involved with theory and analysis than with arithmetic, his handouts and course texts generally provide the necessary visualizations to support his teaching style.

Indeed, his kind, patient manner has probably reassured hundreds of students over the years and communicated complex concepts to the most resistant. "Like any teacher," he says, "I think the best part is when someone gets it and you know they get it and they are so pleased to get it. That's very rewarding."

When he is not teaching, Baggett plays the piano, enjoys a good mystery novel, and takes long walks with his mathematician wife, whom he credits with much of his success and happiness. Most of his time, he admits, is involved with work and the students and faculty he meets at school.

"The academic life is a good life," he says. "You are with bright, interesting people. The work is always different and new."

Despite his honest appraisal of difficulties, Baggett says that teaching mathematics has been rich with rewards. First, there is the gratifying moment of knowing that another human being has grasped the information he is hoping to get across, and then, there is the personal wealth of friendship with students and faculty alike that stretches over 31 years and thousands of miles.

SALARY: After 31 years, $65,000 for nine months' teaching, "high for this university, but average for the entire country."

EQUIPMENT USED: *For mobility:* a long cane. *For teaching preparation and research:* a computer with a DECtalk speech synthesizer at home and Accent speech synthesizer at work; EMACSPEAK screen-reading software at home, JAWS at work; TEX typesetting software for converting words to Greek characters and mathematics symbols; an Optacon; a manual typewriter; a Perkins Brailler; and an audio-cassette recorder.

ABOUT VIRGIL A. COOK

HOME
Blacksburg, Virginia

SCHOOL
Virginia Tech

AGE
62

CAUSE OF VISUAL IMPAIRMENT
A damaged optic nerve from a birth injury

VISUAL ACUITY
Total blindness

ASSOCIATE PROFESSOR OF ENGLISH

Virgil A. Cook

"I love my job. It's wonderful to be able to talk about all these marvelous writers and get paid for it!"

WHEN VIRGIL A. COOK was a graduate student of English literature preparing to look for a job, he had some good instincts about psychology, too. It was the 1960s, and he knew that it might be difficult to gain acceptance as a blind professor.

At Virginia Tech, however, there was already a blind man on staff—a highly respected man who had begun as the secretary to the YMCA and had later taken on other responsibilities. Paul Derring had been a regular speaker at state and regional YMCA conferences, and Virgil Cook had met and admired this significant blind role model when he, Cook, was still a high school student. "He had blazed the trail for me," Cook points out. Here, he believed, where a blind person had already done the work of removing misconceptions, an aspiring English teacher who happened to be blind might just get a fairer hearing. He was right. At his only interview nearly 35 years ago, Cook was offered a job on the spot—the only job he has ever had.

It is a great job, Cook will tell you, one in which a person who loves literature can read and teach it every day. Over the years, he has taught English composition, British literature, American literature, technical writing, and senior seminars on his favorite author, William Faulkner, along with other southern writers like Ellen Glasgow and Flannery O'Connor.

In the early days, Cook depended heavily on braille texts and readers to prepare for class and grade papers. He was among the first of his colleagues to recognize the value of technology, and his job became much easier with computers in the 1980s. He asked students who had access to computers to turn in papers on disk, enabling him to load their work into his computer for direct access to each student's syntax, style, and spelling.

When the department chair read about his use of computers in the university's alumni magazine, he asked Cook to tackle a course in technical writing. That was in 1985, and the class continues to be one of his more popular offerings. Taught entirely by electronic mail, the technical writing course attracts students from a variety of engineering and scientific fields. The "classroom" is an electronic mailing list, where Cook posts assignments and all students post responses.

The most attractive feature of teaching by electronic mail is convenience to the student. Students can "attend class" or post homework from anywhere they have access to a computer and modem. One student, Cook reports, actually posted assignments while visiting relatives in Hong Kong. For Cook, the technical writing course offers the obvious advantages of providing instant access to students' work and inserting comments directly into the text. For papers that need comments throughout, Cook has devised a simple system of placing all comments between braces, thus making it easy for students to search their returned electronic text for feedback. Another hidden plus for a blind teacher, Cook says, is that he always knows immediately which student is writing.

"I never really developed a knack for learning all their voices," he says—and no wonder. With at least three new classes of 25–35 students each per semester, learning every voice is probably not feasible for anyone. Students generally sit in the same places, however, and beyond that, Cook's preference has been to avoid the possibility of stifling discussion by forcing students to identify themselves.

"I move around somewhat during lectures when I'm not reading directly from a text," he explains, "but I often sit on the edge of the desk because the physical closeness to the students encourages more participation."

His method of acquiring necessary texts in braille has changed dramatically over the years. Whereas he once listened to novels on audiotape and took extensive braille notes to work from in class, Cook now uses a scanner with optical character recognition for importing necessary pages into his computer and printing them out in braille. Many works—from British romantic poetry to American novels—can be found on the Internet and downloaded as complete texts. Cook has become an expert in searching the Internet to locate and capture literary works in this way.

From the beginning, Cook has been quick to recognize ways in which technology could make his job easier. A secretary sends him class rosters electronically, and he submits his grades in the same way. Although he once employed students as readers for a variety of tasks, he now finds that most paperwork can be handled independently with technology.

All his equipment has been purchased by the university. Whether other institutions are as supportive as his has been is by no means certain, but Cook recognizes his good fortune. "Virginia Tech was supporting people with disabilities long before the law required it," he says. Every year or so, funding becomes available for certain kinds of projects and equipment for faculty, and Cook uses those opportunities to request new pieces of adaptive technology.

He has always lived within walking distance of campus, he says, so that most of the time his own feet provide transportation. Although he is not always in the same classroom, his courses are generally scheduled in the same building. When he was occasionally assigned to a building a distance away on campus, he says he adjusted his style from briefcase to backpack to make carrying his equipment more feasible.

Other than pointing out to students at the beginning of each semester that "if you raise your hand, you'll be holding it up till next week" to get a response, he rarely discusses his blindness. Students see that he uses a long cane and reads from braille texts, but his blindness is not a topic of discussion. Nor has it created any problems in the classroom. At this stage, he points out, students are usually present because they want to learn, so discipline is not an issue. His examinations are always essays, which eliminates the opportunity to cheat. The honor code at Virginia Tech is such that to witness cheating and fail to report it is as much a violation of ethics as to be the culprit, so on the few occasions when he has suspected dishonesty in the classroom, a student has usually confirmed his suspicion by reporting the offense. For the most part, classroom management is not something he gives much thought to. He has never felt the need for a teaching assistant or aide in the classroom.

Today, there is a building named for the man who "blazed the trail" for Cook over 30 years ago. Clearly, with his forays into technology and creative approaches to teaching, Cook has blazed a trail for others as well. His son and daughter are both adults now with lives of their own, but the Cooks are a close family "in the kitchen spoiling the broth," as his whimsical telephone message warmly greets callers, and he and his wife continue to share many interests beyond education and literature. For decades, they have sung in both church and community choirs together, particularly enjoying the performance of classical works such as masses and requiems by Bach, Mozart, and Handel. Furthermore, his love of literature and reading continue to be a major force in his life and one for which he has been recognized by peers.

In 1998, Dr. Virgil Cook was honored by Virginia Tech with a lifetime achievement award and, yes, for blazing a trail. His technical writing course was the first of its kind to be taught entirely on-line via electronic mail, and his pioneering efforts with this course and other technological ventures have benefited many.

"I love my job," he says simply. "It's wonderful to be able to talk about all these marvelous writers and get paid for it!"

SALARY: $45,000 for nine months of teaching, and an additional salary for teaching summer school.

EQUIPMENT USED: *For mobility:* a long cane. *For teaching preparation and research:* a Pentium computer with JAWS for Windows and DOS, a DECtalk speech synthesizer, an Arkenstone Open Book reading system, a Versapoint braille embosser; Braille 'n Speak, a laser printer, a Perkins Brailler, and a 19-cell braille slate and stylus always in his coat pocket.

ABOUT JOHN W. SMITH

HOME
Athens, Ohio

SCHOOL
Ohio University

AGE
38

CAUSE OF VISUAL IMPAIRMENT
Congenital glaucoma and an injury at age three

VISUAL ACUITY
Total blindness

PROFESSOR OF SPEECH COMMUNICATIONS
John W. Smith

"The whole business of verbal and nonverbal communication, spoken words and body language, and connecting human beings has always fascinated me."

"I T WAS 1979, and I was a sophomore at Indiana University," reminisces John W. Smith, professor of speech communications at Ohio University in Athens. "I had changed my major five times and didn't know what I wanted to do. Then it happened. I was sitting in Dr. Camille Schuster's Business and Professional Communications course, and it hit me: This is what I want to do."

Once that decision was made, the determined young student used his energy, intelligence, and positive outlook on life to propel him down the path toward achieving his goal. It would not be long before he was a graduate assistant at Purdue University, pursuing two master's degrees; a doctoral student at Wayne State University in Detroit, where he earned his Ph.D.; and then a faculty member. In his

14 years of teaching, he has conveyed his love of communications to countless students.

When it comes to pursuing and being chosen for new jobs, Smith says that he has always been in an advantageous position. He has always had a good job when interviewing for another, and the self-assurance that situation creates has served him well. For the past five years, he has worked as a professor of speech communications in the School of Inter-personal Communications at Ohio University. (The field of speech communications incorporates all aspects of communicating with the public, including public performance, rhetoric, clarity of content, and electronic media.) He took that job, he says, because his interviewers treated him with so much respect and dignity that he wanted to be in such a positive environment daily.

As a beginning teacher, Smith taught public speaking, listening to "a hundred speeches a day about cats and dogs and recycling," he quips, but with education and experience, he moved on to more advanced communications courses. To date, he has taught courses in persuasion, interpersonal communications, political communications, speech making before 1945, speech making after 1945, great black communicators, and others. In his Communication in Campaigns course, students conduct an entire campaign—writing speeches, public service announcements, printed flyers, and other promotional materials—which actually benefits a political candidate or nonprofit agency in the community.

His classes are lively and contemporary, his students are involved, and Smith speaks passionately about his chosen field. "I just love the whole process of communication," he says with characteristic intensity and energy. "The whole business of verbal and nonverbal communication, spoken words and body language, and connecting human beings has always fascinated me." To do his job as a blind person, Smith says, has required adaptations not unlike those in other areas of life. "You find ways; you figure things out as you go along," he says.

When his course load was focused more on public speaking, on evaluating both verbal and non-verbal delivery, he developed an array of techniques for getting the job done. He would position himself near his desk so he could hear slight movements, such as a student looking down at notes, shuffling papers, or shuffling feet. By using peer evaluations, he encouraged students to focus on the visual aspects of their classmates' presentations and thus fill in the gaps where feedback was more difficult for him to provide. He used videotapes that were reviewed by sighted evaluators or sighted and in-class monitors—whatever it took to get the job done.

Although Smith still requires his students to do some public speaking, believing that the ability to speak to a group is essential for a successful communications career, evaluating students' speeches is now a small part of his teaching job. With the advanced-level courses he teaches, he has essays and reaction papers to evaluate, campaign strategies to discuss and measure, and research approaches to review with a few doctoral candidates.

To manage these tasks, Smith uses various types of equipment and techniques. Computers, sighted readers, and one-on-one meetings with students are all part of his day's work. Recently, he has discovered the ease and independence of receiving via electronic mail the reaction papers that each student in his Black Communication Styles course is required to write as a spontaneous response to a public speech of his or her choice.

The best part of the job, Smith says, is always connecting with people at various points in their lives. It is a life of learning, listening, and meeting new people. "There's no time to get bored," he laughs, "and if there is, the quarter's over and it's time to start a new class, meet new people, start all over again."

The university has been generous, he says, offering from the start to provide whatever equipment is necessary for him to do the job. At work, he has the usual arsenal of equipment used by blind professionals—a Perkins Brailler, Braille 'n Speak, a computer, an Arkenstone Open Book reading system, and an audiocassette recorder. Although the university would supply an assistant in the classroom, he has rarely felt the need for one.

"In the area of interpersonal communications," he explains, "you have to be 'out there' all the time. Personality is important, and you need to be self-confident in every move you make. If my blindness or my blackness ever becomes the issue in my teaching, then I'm not doing my job."

This is not to say that he denies his visual impairment. At the beginning of each quarter, he offers his students an explanation of his blindness and an opportunity to ask questions. He talks easily about his blindness throughout his relationship with students, believing that some vulnerability in this regard sends the clear message that it is OK to talk about it. Students have mentioned over time that because he does not use the chalkboard or overheads in his teaching, to listen to him is like "listening to a story," and that attending his lectures without the addition of eye contact has made them pay attention more closely. Although fascinating discussions arise surrounding blindness, Smith emphasizes that the focus of his teaching is communication.

When asked about discrimination, he reiterates how fortunate he has been in finding jobs. "Sure," he says, "somewhere, sometime, there may have been some discrimination. But if a person ignores me because of my blindness, I just move on to the next person."

Living just two miles (three kilometers) from the campus, Smith finds it easy to get rides to work most of the time—with his wife, a neighbor, or colleagues. Although he usually spends long hours at the office, his goal is to begin to work more in his home office so he can spend more time with his two young daughters.

"It's a great life, and I'd recommend the job to anyone," he says, "but with certain reservations. You have to be unafraid to take risks, self-confident enough to put yourself out there every day, and know that it is *work!*"

SALARY: After 14 years, $50,000 for nine months of teaching; for summer courses about 20 percent more.

EQUIPMENT USED: *For mobility:* a long cane. *For teaching preparation and research:* an IBM computer with a DECtalk speech synthesizer, an Arkenstone Open Book reading system, Braille 'n Speak, a Perkins Brailler, and audiocassette recorders.

MUSIC EDUCATION

ABOUT CHRISTINA COOKE

HOME
Newberg, Oregon

SCHOOL
Open Bible Christian School

AGE
32

CAUSE OF VISUAL IMPAIRMENT
Retinopathy of prematurity (related to premature birth)

VISUAL ACUITY
Light perception

MUSIC TEACHER
Christina Cooke

" . . . I've never worried about discipline. The whole issue here of behavior is about character building: You behave well whether a person can see you or not."

CHRISTINA COOKE was in the seventh grade when she decided it was time to get serious about practicing the piano. Later, for a school assignment, she observed and interviewed the woman who would serve as the role model for her chosen career as a piano teacher. She was old enough to know that to teach music, one needs to be a musician.

The piano and flute have been integral companions in her life since she made that decision, but her career goal has been considerably expanded. After graduating from George Fox University in her hometown of Newberg, Oregon, in 1987, Cooke began to build her private piano-teaching business. That business went well enough, but she soon realized that piano students came after school, which left her restless during school hours.

"I was a bit concerned about my hirability in public schools," she recalls. "Their music budgets are always being cut, and I thought I might need an aide."

111

Then conversations with a friend led to news of children in a church-related school that did not have a music program. Cooke submitted a proposal, and by January 1988 she was on the staff of the Open Bible Christian School to initiate a music curriculum for students from kindergarten through grade 12.

For children in kindergarten through the fourth grade, Cooke provides a general music program. The children are involved in singing, music notation basics, and music theory. In the third grade, everyone learns to play the recorder.

Students in grades 5–12 are in the band and choir, and although these classes are optional, nearly everyone in school participates. The choir students learn to sing two- and three-part music, mostly sacred music, she says, with some spirituals and an occasional popular song for fun. The music for the bands includes an eclectic mix of marches, spirituals, and ragtime, and the arrangements range from simple for beginning students to complicated for experienced students.

When Cooke came to the job, there was an old record player and a chalkboard. "I didn't use one and couldn't use the other," she says. There was no supply of musical scores to draw from and little money in the budget to build a library. Welcoming the challenge, Cooke improvised; she wrote simple melodies for her recorder students and wrote her own arrangements for the choir and bands.

With the Eureka A4, an Australian computer with speech output and a braille-style keyboard, Cooke could type her musical compositions and produce printed scores for her students to read. Today, she has an abundance of band and choir books for her students to use. To transcribe the music for herself, she uses musically talented high school students to dictate from printed scores, naming the values of the notes and playing the notes on the piano. Cooke transcribes the music into braille, binds each score, labels the cover in braille, and adds it to her growing alphabetical library of teaching materials.

Using the shareware program Grade Guide on her computer, Cooke can enter grades in a number of categories—practice, performance, quizzes, behavior, or coming to class prepared—and then ask the program to calculate the overall grade in a variety of ways. Results can be printed out for individual students, saved to a file for Cooke's own use later, or simply viewed on the screen.

In a student body of under 200 students in all, the classes are small and usually easy to manage. Only for the combined fifth–sixth-grade choir of 23 students does Cooke feel the need for a little sighted support. During that class, a room monitor—another teacher or volunteer parent—pops in and out of the room to help maintain discipline. Otherwise, Cooke says, she feels little need for anyone else to be present with her and her students. If a classroom teacher wants to remain in the music room to grade papers or simply to listen to the music, that is OK, too.

Students' questions about blindness, Cooke says, come naturally and are comfortably handled. "Older kids have had me for years," she comments, "so they're used to me and don't ask questions often. The younger children have lots of questions, and they're fun to answer."

They want to know everything from how she dresses in the morning and selects her clothes to how she shops, uses her dog, or cooks dinner at night. She answers pragmatically, with facts and clear explanations. When an older child asks, upon being disciplined to sit straight, how she knew he was leaning back in his chair, she responds: "My ears work pretty well. I knew you were leaning back because your voice was bouncing off the ceiling."

All the children love her dog guide, a creamy yellow Labrador named Doc, and fully understand how he works for her. At the end of each class, the younger children line up at the door and give Doc two pats each on the way out.

When she takes her choir or band students to music festivals—at nearby George Fox University or a few hundred miles away in Seattle—parents eagerly volunteer to come along as chaperons. "The whole school has just been wonderfully supportive," she says of parents and teachers alike. "And that's one of the reasons I've never worried about discipline. The whole issue here of behavior is about character building: You behave well whether a person can see you or not."

Cooke's style of teaching is to circulate as much as possible and hear each student closely. If a student is not singing, she moves in close and sings at him or her. It is a simple technique that always works.

Despite her full-time school position, Cooke never relinquished her original goal. She goes home to her private studio each day, where she teaches private piano students until about 6 P.M.

"They're like family," she says of the piano students who have had her individualized attention once every week, sometimes for as long as six or seven years. "I hear about what's going on in the rest of their lives, and I'm really interested."

Although she says that a full day of teaching music leaves her too "musicked out" for daily practice of her own, there is still music in her hours away from school and her home studio. Cooke conducts a handbell choir at her church and gives community performances on both the flute and piano. She has self-published a small book of compositions, *Hymns for Solo and Duet Instruments,* which has sold well to other Christian schools. In her free time, she also likes to knit, read, and ride on her tandem bike.

She is lucky, Cooke believes, to have created her own job and to be strongly supported by the entire school staff. But the best part, she says, "is uncovering the talent that God has given these children and nurturing it."

SALARY: $20,000 for 10 months of teaching.

EQUIPMENT USED: *For mobility:* her yellow Labrador, Doc, from Guide Dogs for the Blind, San Rafael, California. *For word processing:* an IBM-compatible computer with an Artic speech board and a Touch Window that was designed as shareware and is not widely distributed, a CD-ROM drive, a shareware program called Grade Guide, and a Perkins Brailler. *For composing and transcribing music:* a Eureka A4 personal computer.

SPECIAL EDUCATION

ABOUT CAROL McCARL

HOME
Salem, Oregon

SCHOOL
Oregon School for the Blind

AGE
58

CAUSE OF VISUAL IMPAIRMENT
Retinitis pigmentosa

VISUAL ACUITY
Light perception

TEACHER OF BLIND AND VISUALLY IMPAIRED CHILDREN

Carol McCarl

"The joy in teaching is the difference that you see in kids whom you met five months or five years ago, the changes that you know you made happen; because you were there, you helped them learn a new skill and believe in themselves."

THE OPERATIVE WORD in Carol McCarl's 35 years of teaching may well be *change*. McCarl set out to be an academic classroom teacher, teaching the basic primary and elementary curriculum to children who are blind or visually impaired. She ended up literally on the other side of the country from where she began, teaching life skills and problem solving to children of all ages with a multitude of additional difficulties.

Legally blind since early childhood because of retinitis pigmentosa, McCarl was a student at the residential Wisconsin School for the Blind. She remembers fondly her eagerness to learn to read braille as a first grader and her early commitment to share her love of learning with other children.

After four years of itinerant teaching in Connecticut, she took a job at the Oregon School for the Blind in 1964, because of her personal feeling that she would have greater control over how and what children were learning.

"I feel you can't teach a child when you're on a bus or in a taxi," she says of those days in Connecticut when she was always on the road. She remembers her early frustration with giving a suggestion to a classroom teacher who had only one blind child and then coming back the following week to repeat the same lesson and suggestion all over again.

Ironically, after a few years of teaching first- and then sixth-grade classes at the Oregon School for the Blind, McCarl found herself on the road again. From 1973 to 1983, she traveled to four Oregon counties, providing services to children in rural areas for whom the State School for the Blind was legally responsible. It was then that she began to worry deeply about the quality of services and socialization available to children who were spread out in public school districts without peers or role models who were blind or visually impaired.

The same year that her job brought her back to the residential school, McCarl established a nonprofit organization for publishing a magazine for blind and visually impaired young people. "I felt that I'd abandoned all those kids in rural areas when I came back to school," she says now of her passion to establish Blindskills and launch the *Lifeprints* magazine. "The only other blind person any of those kids ever saw was me, and half the time, they didn't believe that I was blind, that a blind person could be a teacher!"

Thus began her double career: teacher by day and magazine publisher in the evenings and on weekends. Her daytime teaching assignment had changed yet again, and she had found a new way of teaching children throughout the country and beyond through the pages of a magazine just for them.

In the 1980s, McCarl began to use a style of teaching that was far different from her early traditional classroom preparation at Boston University and the Perkins School for the Blind. Technically, her responsibilities were to teach social studies, English, and keyboarding skills to junior and senior high school students. In reality, she says, much of her time was devoted to teaching basic life skills to children who were blind or had multiple disabilities. "My goal was to teach them to use the brain they had to do ordinary things."

McCarl cites example after example of students who graduated from public high schools, equipped, she feels, with a diploma and little else. "Blind people need so much to use their hands," she says fervently and with concern for the many children who frequently are missing such training in public schools. For example, a student who thought she knew how to use the keyboard fully had actually only learned to use two fingers to play a game. McCarl's task was to teach her better keyboarding skills—to type letters and envelopes for daily survival.

In her problem-solving class, the students worked through such scenarios as how to shop for and prepare food, organize clothing, or plan a trip to and from a job interview. An all-day project might be to coach one student through the process of making telephone calls to get the right pieces of information to put together a bus route for a necessary trip downtown.

Her classroom, she says, often represented two extremes. "They were the 'misfits,' the ones with low self-esteem who didn't know they could be anything or anybody, or they were the ones who had been told so often how bright they were but didn't know that it was important to face someone while speaking to them." McCarl had a reputation for never giving up, and this quality stands her in good stead with these and other students. The nature of classes in schools for blind children often tends to lean toward diversity. Numbers in residential schools frequently are small and disabilities in addition to blindness are so varied that classes representing extremes are more common than in larger student populations.

Also with the 1980s came a voluminous amount of paperwork, the one aspect of teaching that McCarl never learned to like (she is not reluctant to say that she prefers spending time with the students). With the same Apple IIe and IIc she used to teach her students, she prepared an Individualized Education Program for each student in the fall and spring that included such goals as learning to read better, write a sentence, count money, and make a bed.

In 1990, McCarl added another magazine to her publishing venture. *Dialogue,* a Chicago-based magazine that had delivered information and encouragement to blind adults for three decades, was about to collapse, and McCarl came to the rescue. Today, her two magazines are combined into one publication—entitled *Dialogue*—designed to teach and foster self-esteem and independence among blind and visually impaired adolescents and adults.

After officially retiring from the Oregon School for the Blind in 1994, McCarl has never stopped teaching. She is a frequent substitute teacher and rents office space for Blindskills from the school. Students now get work experience under her instruction that is not unlike the teaching she has done for years. One student may be responsible for going to a nearby café to pick up lunch for McCarl's part-time accountant. Another student may improve her braille skills and learn to alphabetize and organize as McCarl directs her through the process of building a braille resource file on four-by-six-inch (10-by-15-cm) cards, to be used by the Blindskills staff. Others collate, stuff envelopes, or learn to run the vacuum in the Blindskills office.

Like every teacher, McCarl has learned over the years, too. She takes as much pride in helping one student work, section by section, to earn his General Equivalency Diploma as in teaching another to operate a manual can opener. The latter student was a bright high school graduate who spoke two languages fluently but had not learned to do anything with his hands. "I'd put the can opener and a new empty can on his desk," she recalls, "and I'd hear him working at it and working at it. I can still hear the can lid hit his desktop and his exclamation, 'I did it!' And I knew that what he also meant was 'If I can do this one thing with my hands, then I'm going to be OK.'

"The joy in teaching is the difference that you see in kids whom you met five months or five years ago, the changes that you know you made happen; because you were there, you helped them learn a new skill and believe in themselves."

SALARY: About $30,000 for teaching four days per week, nine months per year.

EQUIPMENT USED: *For mobility:* a long cane. *For teaching preparation:* a Perkins Brailler, slate and stylus, Braille 'n Speak, Apple IIe and IIc computers, and audiocassette recorders.

ABOUT GILLIE PRESLEY

HOME
Tuscaloosa, Alabama

SCHOOL
Faucett Destavia Elementary School

AGE
46

CAUSE OF VISUAL IMPAIRMENT
Congenital cataracts

VISUAL ACUITY
No usable sight in right eye; 20/400 (6/120 [its metric equivalent]) in left eye

LEARNING DISABILITIES TEACHER
Gillie Presley

"I love my job. It's so wonderful teaching kids when they really learn something, when they really have it; it's so much fun."

FOR CHILDREN who have difficulty processing written information in the same ways as do other children, Gillie Presley serves as a daily living example of how people can read and write in a variety of ways while being productive and successful grown-ups.

For 20 years, Presley has given the fourth, fifth, and sixth graders who have been diagnosed with learning disabilities in Faucett Destavia, a Tuscaloosa public elementary school, the additional help they need as well as some additional between-the-lines lessons.

Teaching primarily mathematics, reading, and spelling to 20 or more students per year, Presley uses whatever technique works best for individual children. She reads from a braille mathematics textbook and then writes on the chalkboard. She has students read aloud to her from their reading text and assists them according to what she hears.

As approaches to special education have shifted over the years, so has Presley's style of teaching.

Today, she has her own classroom, in which she teaches students in small groups throughout the day. In keeping with the move toward full inclusion, she accompanies three students to the larger mathematics class and helps them to whatever degree is necessary for them to participate with the other children. A team-teaching approach is used for the inclusion plan: Presley and a regular classroom teacher alternate teaching mathematics lessons to the entire fourth grade on different days. After a lesson has been presented to the whole class, Presley then gives individualized attention to her students with learning disabilities. Sometimes she has to read the word problems to them; at other times the exercise seems overwhelming to them, so she modifies the lesson.

Teaching in the same elementary school for 20 years, Presley says, has been a comfortable situation. The rest of the faculty have always been supportive, which has made both teaching and personal adaptations less complicated.

For the first time this year, Presley has an aide in the classroom all day. Before, an aide was available only for about an hour each day. Presley has always paid her own readers, but this year, the aide reads and grades papers one hour each day.

A former student of the Alabama School for the Blind, Presley says that she is grateful to have learned braille as a first grader. Although her vision was sufficient for traveling without a long cane or other device until a year or so ago, it was never deemed good enough for reading large print. Presley learned cursive writing shortly before she enrolled at Troy State University in Troy, Alabama. She knew by the 10th grade, she says, that she liked children and wanted to teach. It was not until she earned her master's degree in special education that she decided to concentrate her energies in the area of learning disabilities.

"Learning disabilities was an open field, and schools were hiring a lot of people," Presley recalls. "I thought it might be easier to get a job—and it was." She sent applications to school districts throughout Alabama and got friends or relatives to drive her to all the interviews. Some schools probably ruled her out because of her visual impairment, she says, but none discriminated against her overtly. She received three firm offers simultaneously in 1977 and chose the one in her hometown, Tuscaloosa. She has never regretted it.

Learning disabilities is a stimulating area of education, Presley believes, because the children are at many different levels of learning. Some are both gifted and learning disabled; others have attention difficulties or behavioral problems. Every child is a challenge.

On the first day of school, she talks to the children about her blindness. From then on, she says, questions come up naturally, and she answers them as they arise. For the most part, her visual impairment is rarely talked about. Children know she cannot see well and take it for granted that she reads braille. Occasionally, some children tell her their feelings were hurt because she did not wave back to them at the mall or other places outside school. "They know I don't see well at school," she laughs, "but somehow that doesn't transfer for them to the mall."

Presley's philosophy regarding accommodations is that she knew she had a disability when she applied for the job and to ask for costly additions after she was hired would be inappropriate. "I know our school district is in a financial hole," she says, "and it wouldn't be fair to ask for money to be spent on me that should be spent on a child."

This does not mean that she has never received accommodations. Two years ago, she wrote a letter requesting computer equipment, explaining how much more effective she would be with the technological assistance. She believes the school granted her request, no questions asked, because she had never asked for accommodations in the past.

With the new computer equipment, Presley can scan pages from reading texts and other handouts and then print them out in braille. (Mathematics textbooks have to be purchased in braille, she says, because their formats do not scan well. However, because the school is using new mathematics textbooks this year that are not yet available in braille, Presley transcribes upcoming pages into braille each afternoon from her aide's dictation.) She also uses the computer to prepare tests and work sheets. In some situations she uses the computer directly with the students. The talking computer is ideal for a visually impaired teacher to teach keyboarding skills, for example, since it provides immediate feedback when a student makes an error. For a particularly slow reader, she has found that an effective teaching technique is to scan a story and have the computer read it aloud while a student reads from the book.

Working with fourth, fifth, and sixth graders in small groups has several advantages in regard to accommodations, too. If Presley does not have written material in braille, she simply asks a student to read it. Students generally feel important doing so. She is careful, however, when asking the students to read spelling words from one another's papers. "When there's someone they don't like," she laughs, "they'll swear they can't read the handwriting!"

Outside the classroom, Presley's life is filled with activities. In addition to several faculty committees, she is involved in a number of church and civic organizations, including an AIDS Care Team (supporting individuals with AIDS one on one), a lobbying group for poor people, accompanying children on visits to mothers in prisons, and two teachers' sororities. In summer, she works with Project HELP, a five-week program for students with learning disabilities. And she has held office in her high school alumni organization, the National Association of Blind Teachers, and the local chapter of the American Council of the Blind.

"I love my job," she says. "It's so wonderful teaching kids when they really learn something, when they really have it; it's so much fun. Sometimes, if you show them one way of doing something, they'll show you another way that works, and you realize they're teaching you. It's a constant challenge and it's fun!"

SALARY: $32,000 for nine months of teaching.

EQUIPMENT USED: *For mobility:* a long cane. *For teaching preparation:* an Arkenstone Open Book reading system; a computer with Vocal-Eyes screen-reading software, a DECtalk speech synthesizer, and Megadots braille translation software; an Index braille embosser; a standard ink-jet printer; and a Perkins Brailler.

ABOUT OLIVIA CHAVEZ SCHONBERGER

HOME
El Paso, Texas

SCHOOL
Texas Education Service Center, Region 19

AGE
47

CAUSE OF VISUAL IMPAIRMENT
Retinoblastoma, onset at age two

VISUAL ACUITY
Total blindness

EDUCATIONAL FACILITATOR–PROJECT MANAGER OF SERVICES FOR STUDENTS WHO HAVE VISUAL IMPAIRMENTS

Olivia Chavez Schonberger

"What I love about my job is that it's never static."

WHEN OLIVIA Chavez Schonberger was a first-year college student at the University of Texas at Austin, her primary goal was to become an interpreter for the United Nations. Languages came easily to her, and she loved adventure.

Her college advisers had other ideas. She would need to learn to read and write, not just speak, languages, they told her, and she would have to be fluent in six languages, not just the three that she already knew. Furthermore, since she would need to handle confidential information, it would be dangerous to hire her because the information would have to be conveyed to her through a sighted reader.

The first alternative suggested to her was that she teach a foreign language. "I knew I didn't want to do that," Schonberger says. "My mother's native language was Spanish, and I knew how impatient I'd been teaching her English. Teaching a language was not for me."

Like so many students, she switched majors several times, until she was finally forced to make a decision. In the end, she received a bachelor's degree in elementary education, including certification in teaching students with visual impairments. Later, she obtained a master's degree in school counseling from the University of Texas at El Paso.

After a stint of rehabilitation teaching for adults and youths, she learned of a job in her hometown, El Paso. In 1977, she was hired as the first teacher consultant to schools in Region 19. In 1980, she was made coordinator of the growing department, supervising two other full-time teachers and managing an annual budget of $250,000.

Among Schonberger's many direct responsibilities is hands-on instruction of children from birth to 22 years. Her territory includes 12 schools and 125 children. In a typical week, she may visit parents of children with multiple disabilities and help work out ways of fostering the children's physical, mental, and sensory development. She may install a computer system in a school and teach the children and teachers how to use the adaptive software that provides it with speech or braille output. Or she may attend a meeting for a student's Individualized Education Program, run an in-service faculty training program for staff in a school that has its first visually impaired student, or write a grant proposal to bring in professors (from Texas Tech University

136

in Lubbock, 400 miles [645 km] away) to conduct workshops for teachers on the basics of blindness.

"What I love about my job is that it's never static," says the upbeat, energetic Schonberger. "I get to travel a lot. I still get to work with kids and parents, and I'm always interacting with teachers and other school staff. I just love it."

To do her job, she makes use of much of the adaptive technology available to blind people. In her office, she uses an Arkenstone Open Book reading system and a computer with a DECtalk speech synthesizer and JAWS for DOS and Windows. For note taking while traveling from school to school, she uses a Braille Lite.

Because her job frequently involves recommending, ordering, and installing computer equipment and training children and teachers to use it, her knowledge extends far beyond the equipment she uses in her office. She is familiar with Keynote Gold, Doubletalk, Vocal-Eyes, and other access software.

All her equipment has been purchased by her employer. She is also provided with a driver 16 hours per week who does some reading for her and a secretarial pool for clerical assistance.

"If a school wants me there," she explains, "and my driver is not available to me, they're all really accommodating. They'll often just send someone to pick me up."

In-service programs for teachers are particularly gratifying, Schonberger says, because the teachers are so responsive and interested to know how to serve a blind student appropriately. "I recently went to a school where the principal had called in everyone—not just the teachers, but the janitor and the cafeteria staff and everyone—so they would all learn how to do the sighted guide technique and best help a visually impaired kid. . . . I just love that."

As fast-paced and busy as her job can get, however, there are the quieter spells when she visits families in rural areas, particularly those whose children have multiple disabilities. Reviewing a morning spent with a four-year-old who is both nonverbal and unable to move, she illustrates how she becomes involved with families: "He can't speak yet, but we think he understands. So I helped give his mother some ideas of things to do that can reinforce language for him—have him touch the diaper when she changes it, touch the spoon to his mouth and say "spoon," so he can associate the object with what happens next. . . . Then there's some counseling, too. This particular mother worries about leaving her child, so I encouraged her to leave him alone at school a few hours each week, to practice letting go."

Because she is an administrator, Schonberger also spends portions of her time managing budgets, supervising staff, writing grants, and purchasing equipment. Many of these things, she says, were areas in which she had no previous experience but learned to do along the way."

Unlike that of a typical teaching job, Schonberger's work schedule is 230 days per year, roughly 11 months. The schedule is a good one, though, with days off every month and liberal vacation time.

"When I was in college and had suddenly to change direction," she recalls now, "I think this probably was my last choice. Some people said that blind people shouldn't teach blind people. But the more resistance I got, the more I wanted to do it."

Indeed, as role model for children and confidence builder for parents, this teacher-administrator goes far beyond the job. A political activist, she has fought for the rights of homeless women and the right of blind people to vote independently. She is active in the field of blindness in a number of organizations, boards, and commissions and was named an Outstanding Ex by her alma mater, Bowie High School, and a Woman of Influence in 1991 by the National Council of Jewish Women.

Olivia Chavez Schonberger still loves languages and adventure. In her job as a teacher and administrator, she has discovered unexpected ways to build on those passions.

SALARY: $46,000 for about 11 months of teaching.

EQUIPMENT USED: *For mobility:* a long cane. *For work-related tasks:* a computer with a DECtalk speech synthesizer and JAWS software, Braille Lite, an Arkenstone Open Book reading system, an Optacon, and audiocassette recorders.

RESOURCES

A wide variety of organizations and companies dis-
seminate information, distribute adaptive equipment, and provide various forms of assistance to
people who are blind or visually impaired, their families, and the professionals who work with them.
This section contains a sample listing of these organizations and companies that may be of particular
usefulness to readers interested in the area of education. Additional information can be found in the
*Directory of Services for Blind and Visually Impaired Per-
sons in the United States and Canada,* published by
the American Foundation for the Blind.

SOURCES OF INFORMATION

National Organizations

The three national organizations listed in this section provide a wide variety of services, including
information and referral. The American Foundation
for the Blind's Careers and Technology Information
Bank is a nationwide database of blind and visually
impaired people who mentor others seeking advice
on careers. The National Association of Blind Educators, a division of the National Federation of the

Blind, and the National Association of Blind Teachers, an affiliate chapter of the American Council of the Blind, are membership organizations for blind and visually impaired teachers.

Careers and Technology Information Bank
American Foundation for the Blind
11 Penn Plaza, Suite 300
New York, NY 10001
(212) 502-7600 or (800) 232-5463
TDD: (212) 502-7662
FAX: (212) 502-7777
E-mail: afbinfo@afb.net
URL: http://www.afb.org

National Association of Blind Educators
c/o National Federation of the Blind
1800 Johnson Street
Baltimore, MD 21230
(410) 659-9314
FAX: (410) 685-5653
E-mail: nfb@access.digex.net
URL: http://www.nfb.org

National Association of Blind Teachers
c/o American Council of the Blind
1155 15th Street, N.W.
Suite 720
Washington, DC 20005
(202) 467-5081 or (800) 424-8666
FAX: (202) 467-5085
E-mail: ncrabb@access.digex.net
URL: http://www.acb.org

Publications

The publications listed below provide invaluable information for teachers. Additional publications are listed in the *AFB Directory of Blind and Visually Impaired Persons in the United States and Canada.*

Dialogue, a quarterly general-interest magazine for people who are visually impaired.
> **c/o Blindskills**
> P.O. Box 5181
> Salem, OR 97304
> (503) 581-4224 or (800) 860-1224
> FAX: (503) 581-0178
> E-mail: blindskl@teleport.com
> URL: http://www.teleport.com/~blindskl

Journal of Visual Impairment & Blindness, a monthly interdisciplinary journal that publishes scholarly information and serves as a forum for the exchange of ideas, the airing of controversies, and the discussion of issues on blindness and visual impairment. The journal includes a news service, which contains such features as "Employment Update," information on employment trends, and "Random Access," a column in which the latest technologies are evaluated.
> **c/o American Foundation for the Blind**
> 11 Penn Plaza, Suite 300
> New York, NY 10001
> (717) 632-3535
> FAX: (717) 633-8920
> URL: http://www.afb.org

TACTIC Magazine, a consumer-oriented quarterly on adaptive technology.
   c/o The Clovernook Center
   Opportunities for the Blind
   7000 Hamilton Avenue
   Cincinnati, OH 45231
   (513) 522-3860 or (888) 234-7156
   FAX: (513) 728-3946

SOURCES OF ADAPTED PRODUCTS AND DEVICES

The following list provides the names of companies and organizations from which adaptive materials and equipment and aids mentioned in this book can be obtained. The EMACSPEAK screen-reading software that is mentioned by Lawrence W. Baggett may be downloaded at no charge from http://www.cs.cornell.edu/home/raman.

AICOM Corporation
2381 Zanker Road, Suite 160
San Jose, CA 95131
(408) 577-0370
FAX: (408) 577-0373
   Accent speech synthesizer

American Printing House for the Blind
P.O. Box 6085, Department 0086
Louisville, KY 40206-0085
(502) 895-2405 or (800) 223-1839
FAX: (502) 895-1509
   slate and stylus (several types)
   National Library Service–compatible
      audiocassette recorder

Arkenstone
555 Oakmead Parkway
Sunnyvale, CA 94086-4023
(408) 245-5900 or (800) 444-4443
FAX: (408) 745-6739
URL: http://www.arkenstone.org
   Arkenstone Open Book reading system

Artic Technologies
55 Park Street, Suite 2
Troy, MI 48083-2753
(810) 588-7370 or (810) 588-1425
FAX: (810) 588-2650
BBS: (810) 588-1424
   Artic SynPhonix speech synthesizer
   Artic TransPort speech synthesizer
   Artic Vision synthetic speech program
   Artic WinVision synthetic speech program

Blazie Engineering
101 East Jerretsville Road
Forest Hill, MD 21050
(410) 893-9333
FAX: (410) 836-5040
URL: http://www.blazie.com
   Braille Blazer embosser
   Braille Lite notetaker
   Braille 'n Speak notetaker

Digital Equipment Corporation
P.O. Box 9501
Merrimac, NH 03054
(800) 344-4825
FAX: (800) 234-2298
   DECtalk speech synthesizer

Enabling Technologies Company
1601 N.E. Braille Place
Jensen Beach, FL 34957
(561) 225-2687 or (800) 777-3687
FAX: (561) 225-3299 or (800) 950-3687
   Romeo braille printer (also distributes other
      embossers and braille-related products)

Esselte Pendaflex Corporation
71 Clinton Road
Garden City, NY 11530
(516) 741-3200
   Dymo braille labeler

Guide Dogs for the Blind
P.O. Box 151200
San Rafael, CA 94915-1200
(415) 499-4000 or (800) 295-4050
FAX: (415) 499-4035

Guiding Eyes for the Blind
611 Granite Springs Road
Yorktown Heights, NY 10598
(914) 245-4204
FAX: (914) 245-1609

GW Micro
725 Airport North Office Park
Fort Wayne, IN 46825
(219) 489-3671
FAX: (219) 489-2608
E-mail: vv@gwmicro.com
URL: http://www.gwmicro.com
   Vocal-Eyes screen-reading program for DOS
   Window-Eyes screen-reading program for
      Windows

146

Henter-Joyce
2100 62nd Avenue, North
St. Petersburg, FL 33702
(813) 528-8900 or (800) 336-5658
FAX: (813) 528-8901
E-mail: info@hj.com
URL: http://www.hj.com
   JAWS (Job Access with Speech) screen-reading
      program for DOS
   JAWS for Windows 3.x and 95 screen-reading
      program for Windows

Howe Press of the Perkins School for the Blind
175 North Beacon Street
Watertown, MA 02172
(617) 924-3490
   Perkins Brailler

HumanWare, Inc.
6245 King Road
Loomis, CA 95650
(916) 652-7253 or (800) 722-3393
FAX: (916) 652-7296
E-mail: infor@humanware.com
URL: http://www.humanware.com
   KeyNote, KeyNote Companion, KeyNote Gold
      speech synthesizer and several other access
      technology products

Kurzweil Educational Systems
411 Waverly Oaks Road
Waltham, MA 02154
(617) 893-8200 or (800) 894-5374
FAX: (617) 893-4157
E-mail: info@kurzweiledu.com
URL: http://www.kurzweiledu.com
   Omni 1000 (OCR system and scanner)

Library of Congress National Library Service (NLS) for the Blind and Physically Handicapped
1291 Taylor Street, N.W.
Washington, DC 20542
(202) 707-5100 or (800) 424-8567
  NLS-compatible audiocassette recorder
    (distributed free of charge to eligible users)
  Combination Machine (plays both cassettes
    and records)

The Lighthouse Inc.
11 East 59th Street
New York, NY 10022
(212) 821-9200 or (800) 334-5497
TDD: (212) 821-9713
FAX: (212) 821-9705
  Dymo braille labeler
  handheld magnifiers
  NLS-compatible audiocassette recorder
  slate and stylus

PulseData International, Inc.
4994 Austell Road
Austell, GA 30001
(888) 734-8439
FAX: (770) 732-8580
E-mail: pulse_data@compuserve.com
  closed-circuit television

Raised Dot Computing
408 South Baldwin Street
Madison, WI 53703
(608) 257-9595 or (608) 241-2498

FAX: (608) 257-4143
URL: http://www.well.com/www/dnavy
MegaDots (braille translator)

The Seeing Eye, Inc.
Washington Valley Road
Morristown, NJ 07960
(201) 539-4425

Sighted Electronics
464 Tappan Road
Northvale, NJ 07646
(201) 767-3977
FAX: (201) 767-0612
E-mail: sightedvillage.ios.com
Index braille embosser

Technologies for the Visually Impaired
9 Nolan Court
Hauppauge, NY 11788
(516) 724-4479
Eureka A4 personal computer

TeleSensory Corporation
P.O. Box 7455
455 North Bernardo
Mountain View, CA 94039-7455
(415) 960-0920 or (800) 286-8484
Fax: (415) 969-9064
URL: http://www.telesensory.com
Index braille embosser
Optacon (Note: TeleSensory Corporation no
longer manufactures the Optacon but
continues to provide service)

T.F.I. Engineering, Inc.
529 Main Street
Boston, MA 02129
(617) 242-7007
  DECtalk speech synthesizer
  talking micrometers
  VersaPoint Braille Embosser (braille printer)
  VersaPoint Duo braille embosser

Xerox Imaging Systems
Adaptive Technology Products
9 Centennial Drive
Peabody, MA 01960
(800) 248-6550
FAX: (508) 977-2148
E-mail: doiron@xis.xerox.com
URL: http://www.xerox.com
  Kurzweil Personal Reader (OCR system and
    scanner)
  Reading Edge (stand-alone OCR system)

About the Author

Deborah Kendrick is an award-winning writer, editor, columnist, and poet. The writer of the column "Alive and Well," which appears weekly in the *Cincinnati Enquirer, Columbus Dispatch,* and other newspapers, she also writes a regular column on family issues for *Dialogue,* a general-interest magazine for adolescents and adults who are blind, and she is also editor of *TACTIC,* a quarterly that focuses on access technology. She has written hundreds of features, editorials, and reviews, many of them on disability-related issues, for *Woman's Day, Parenting, Executive Lifestyles, Marriage and Family,* and many other publications. Author of *Jobs To Be Proud Of: Profiles of Workers Who Are Blind or Visually Impaired,* which was honored with the American Council of the Blind's Vernon Henley Media Award in 1994, she was named a "role model for women" by Women in Communications and recipient of the American Foundation for the Blind's 1993 Access Award. Kendrick, who has been blind since childhood, has received numerous other honors for her efforts as journalist and advocate, including the 1997 Maurice McCracken Peace and Justice Award and the National Easter Seal Society's 1995 Grand EDI Award

151

for Print Journalism. A former educator in both elementary and graduate-level classrooms, she continues her connection with young people through school presentations and in-service workshops for teachers. She has three children and lives in Cincinnati, Ohio.

The mission of the American Foundation for the Blind (AFB) is to enable persons who are blind or visually impaired to achieve equality of access and opportunity that will ensure freedom of choice in their lives.

It is the policy of the American Foundation for the Blind to use in the first printing of its books acid-free paper that meets the ANSI Z39.48 Standard. The infinity symbol that appears above indicates that the paper in this printing meets that standard.